SpringerBriefs in Computer Science

SpringerBriefs present concise summaries of cutting-edge research and practical applications across a wide spectrum of fields. Featuring compact volumes of 50 to 125 pages, the series covers a range of content from professional to academic.

Typical topics might include:

- A timely report of state-of-the art analytical techniques
- A bridge between new research results, as published in journal articles, and a contextual literature review
- A snapshot of a hot or emerging topic
- An in-depth case study or clinical example
- A presentation of core concepts that students must understand in order to make independent contributions

Briefs allow authors to present their ideas and readers to absorb them with minimal time investment. Briefs will be published as part of Springer's eBook collection, with millions of users worldwide. In addition, Briefs will be available for individual print and electronic purchase. Briefs are characterized by fast, global electronic dissemination, standard publishing contracts, easy-to-use manuscript preparation and formatting guidelines, and expedited production schedules. We aim for publication 8–12 weeks after acceptance. Both solicited and unsolicited manuscripts are considered for publication in this series.

**Indexing: This series is indexed in Scopus, Ei-Compendex, and zbMATH **

Pedro Mejia Alvarez • Marcelo Leon Ayala
Susana Ortega Cisneros

Main Memory Management on Relational Database Systems

Springer

Pedro Mejia Alvarez
Computacion
CINVESTAV-Guadalajara
Zapopan, Mexico

Marcelo Leon Ayala
Oracle
Redwood City, CA, USA

Susana Ortega Cisneros
CINVESTAV-Guadalajara
Zapopan, Mexico

ISSN 2191-5768   ISSN 2191-5776 (electronic)
SpringerBriefs in Computer Science
ISBN 978-3-031-13294-0   ISBN 978-3-031-13295-7 (eBook)
https://doi.org/10.1007/978-3-031-13295-7

This Springer imprint is published by the registered company Springer Nature Switzerland AG
The registered company address is: Gewerbestrasse 11, 6330 Cham, Switzerland

*This book is dedicated to my daughter
Carolina Mejia-Moya.*

Preface

Big Data applications has initiated much research to develop systems for supporting low latency execution and real-time data analytics. Existing disk-based systems can no longer offer timely response due to the high access latency to hard disks. The low performance is now also becoming an obstacle for organizations which provide a real-time service (e.g., realtime bidding, advertising, social gaming). For instance, trading companies require to detect sudden changes in the trading prices and react instantly (in several milliseconds), which is impossible to achieve using traditional disk-based processing-storage systems. To meet the strict real-time requirements for analyzing mass amounts of data and servicing requests within milliseconds, an in-memory database system that keeps the data in the random access memory (RAM) all the time is necessary.

Nowadays, there is a trend where memory will eventually replace disk and the role of disks must inevitably become more archival. Also, multi-core processors and the availability of large amounts of main memory at low cost are creating new breakthroughs, making it viable to build in-memory systems where a significant part, of the database fits in memory.

Similarly, there have been significant advances in non-volatile memory (NVM) such as SSD and the recent launch of various NVMs such as phase change memory (PCM). The number of I/O operations per second in such devices is much greater than hard disks. Modern high-end servers have multiple sockets, each of which have tens or hundreds of gigabytes of DRAM, and tens of cores, and in total, a server may have several terabytes of DRAM and hundreds of cores. Moreover, in a distributed environment, it is possible to aggregate the memories from a large number of server nodes to the extent that the aggregated memory is able to keep all the data for a variety of large-scale applications.

Database systems have been increasing their capacity over the last few decades, mainly driven by advances in hardware, availability of large amounts of data, collection of data at an unprecedented rate, emerging applications and so on. The landscape of data management systems is increasingly fragmented based on application domains (i.e., applications relying on relational data, graph-based data, stream data).

In business operations, real-time predictability and high speed is not an option, but a must. Hence every opportunity must be exploited to improve performance, including reducing dependency on the hard disk, adding more memory to make more data resident in the memory, and even deploying an in-memory system where all data can be kept in memory.

Most commercial database vendors have recently introduced in-memory database processing to support large-scale applications completely in memory. Therefore, efficient in-memory data management is a necessity for various applications. Nevertheless, in-memory data management is still at its infancy, and is likely to evolve over the next few years.

In this book, we focus on in-memory Relational Data Base systems; readers are referred to [65] for a survey on disk-based systems.

CINVESTAV-Guadalajara, Mexico   *Pedro Mejia Alvarez*
Oracle, Redwood City California, USA,   *Marcelo Leon Ayala*
CINVESTAV-Guadalajara, Mexico   *Susana Ortega Cisneros*

Acknowledgements

We would like to thank, CONACYT and Secretaría de Innovación, Ciencia y Tecnología del Estado de Jalisco, Mexico, for their support in the project: Centro de Innovación, Desarrollo y Tecnológico y Aplicaciones de Internet de las Cosas. Project No.Jal-2015-C03- 272478.

Contents

Chapter 1
The Memory System

This chapter contains some concepts and techniques used for efficient in-memory data management, including memory hierarchy, non-uniform memory access (NUMA), and non-volatile random access memory (NVRAM). These are the basics on which the performance of In-Memory data management systems heavily rely.

1.1 Von Neumann Architecture

Memory plays a significant role in Von Neumann's computer architecture, shown in figue 1.1 . It is the part of the computer system used to store both the program's data and the program's instructions.

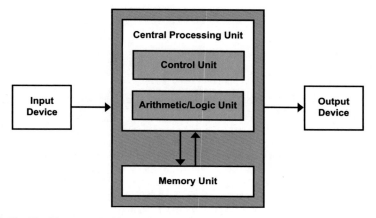

Fig. 1.1 The Von Neumann Architecture

© The Author(s), under exclusive license to Springer Nature Switzerland AG 2022
P. Mejia Alvarez et al., *Main Memory Management on Relational Database Systems*,
SpringerBriefs in Computer Science, https://doi.org/10.1007/978-3-031-13295-7_1

The typical instruction execution cycle of a Von Newman architecture CPU commonly executes the following five stages [1]:

1. Fetch one instruction from memory.
2. Decode the instruction.
3. Fetch the operands of the instruction from memory, if needed.
4. Execute.
5. Save the result of the instruction to memory, if needed.

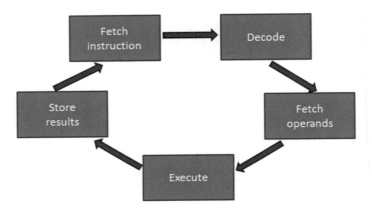

Fig. 1.2 Instruction execution cycle

During the cycle on figure 1.2, the memory system is at least accessed once (on stage 1); however, it can be used multiple times depending on the executing instruction. Frequent accesses is one of the reasons why the memory system is a vital part of the system and a performance sensitive element on the complete computer system.

1.2 Memory

Memory is composed of a large array of bytes [1]. Each Byte in the array has two main characteristics:

1. An address.
2. Each (address) element can be accessed independently from the others.

The sole responsibility of memory is to store or retrieve information at the specified addresses. From the perspective of memory, the only input is a stream of addresses and a control word indicating if the information needs to be read or written at the corresponding address. How the program generates those addresses is not essential: they could come from the program counter, array indexing, indirections, real addresses, among others. That information is irrelevant. The behavior expected from the memory systems is the same: to retrieve the information stored at the specified address.

1.3 Memory Organization

The memory hierarchy is defined in terms of access latency and the logical distance to the CPU. In general, it consists of registers, caches, main memory and disks; from the highest performance to the lowest.

Figure 1.3 shows the typical organization of memory hierarchy. It shows that data access to the higher layers is much faster than to the lower layers, and each of these layers will be introduced in this section.

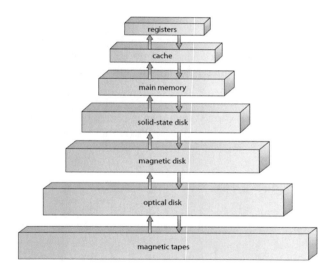

Fig. 1.3 Memory hierarchy

In modern architectures, data cannot be processed by CPU unless it is put in the registers. Thus, data that is about to be processed has to be transmitted through each of the memory layers until it reaches the registers. Consequently, each upper layer serves as a cache for the underlying lower layer to reduce the latency for repetitive data accesses.

A memory hierarchy consist of multiple levels, but data can be copied only between two adjacent levels at a time [2]. The upper level is the one closer to the processor and is smaller and faster than the lower level, since the upper level uses technology that is more expensive.

The minimum unit of information that can be either present or not present in the two-level hierarchy is called a block or a line. If the data requested by the processor appears in some block in the upper level, this is called a hit. If the data is not found in the upper level, the request is called a miss. The lower level in the hierarchy is then accessed to retrieve the block containing the requested data. The hit rate, or hit ratio, is the fraction of memory accesses found in the upper level; it is often used as a measure of the performance of the memory hierarchy. The miss rate is the fraction of memory accesses not found in the upper level.

The performance of a data-intensive program highly depends on the utilization of the memory hierarchy [2]. How to achieve both good spatial and temporal locality is usually what matters the most in the efficiency optimization. In particular, spatial locality assumes that the adjacent data is more likely to be accessed together, whereas temporal locality refers to the observation that it is likely that an item will be accessed again in the near future. Performance is the major reason for having a memory hierarchy, so the time to service hits and misses is important. Hit time is the time to access the upper level of the memory hierarchy, which includes the time needed to determine whether the access is a hit or a miss. The miss penalty is the time to replace a block in the upper level with the corresponding block from the lower level, plus the time to deliver this block to the processor. Because the upper level is smaller and built using faster memory parts, the hit time will be much smaller than the time to access the next level in the hierarchy, which is the major component of the miss penalty.

The concepts used to build memory systems affect many other aspects of a computer, including how the operating system manages memory and I/O, how compilers generate code and even how applications use the computer [5].

1.4 Memory Technologies

There are several primary technologies of memory used nowadays in a modern computer system [2]:

- Register.
- Cache.
- SRAM: Static Random-Access Memory.
- DRAM: Dynamic Random-Access Memory.
- Flash Memory.
- NVM: Non-Volatile Memory.
- Magnetic storage.

Each category of memory has its requirements and can be implemented using different underlying physical technologies. The classification of memory represents an abstraction of memory technologies.

Main memory (SRAM, DRAM, NVM) is also called internal memory, which can be directly addressed and possibly accessed by the CPU, in contrast to external devices such as disks.

1.4.1 Register

A processor register is a small amount of storage within a CPU, on which machine instructions can manipulate directly. In a normal instruction, data is first loaded from the lower memory layers into registers where it is used for arithmetic or test operation, and the result is put back into another register, which is then often stored back into main memory, either by the same instruction or a subsequent one. The length of a register is usually equal to the word length of a CPU, but there also exist double-word, and even wider registers (e.g., 256 bits wide YMMX registers in Intel Sandy Bridge CPU micro architecture), which can be used for single instruction multiple data (SIMD) operations. While the number of registers depends on the architecture, the total capacity of registers is much smaller than that of the lower layers such as cache or memory. However, accessing data from registers is very much faster.

1.4.2 Cache

State of the art processors can execute instructions at a rate of 1 or more per CPU cycle and registers inside the processor are generally accessible by name and within one cycle of the CPU clock. Unfortunately, completing a read or write memory access may take many CPU cycles and the processor normally needs to stall. Main memory and the registers built into the processor itself are the general-purpose storage that the CPU can access directly. Therefore, any instruction that the processor needs to execute and any data required by the instruction must be present in one of these direct access storage devices. They must be in place before the CPU can operate on them, otherwise the instruction needs to be restarted [2]. The usual remedy to prevent the processor from stalling is to add fast memory between the CPU and main memory, typically in the CPU chip. This particular type of memory is called a cache. A cache hit occurs when the instruction or instruction's data is present on the cache when the processor needs it. Otherwise, it is a cache miss. There are several techniques for minimizing the cache miss ratio which will be covered in the next section.

Registers play the role as the storage containers that CPU uses to carry out instructions, while caches act as the bridge between the registers and main memory due to the high transmission delay between the registers and main memory. Cache is made of high-speed static RAM (SRAM) instead of slower and cheaper dynamic RAM (DRAM) that usually forms the main memory. In general, there are three levels of caches, i.e., L1 cache, L2 cache and L3 cache (also called last level cache—LLC), with increasing latency and capacity. L1 cache is further divided into data cache (i.e., L1-dcache) and instruction cache (i.e., L1-icache) to avoid any interference between data access and instruction access.

Cache is typically subdivided into fixed-size logical cache lines, which are the atomic units for transmitting data between different levels of caches and between the last level cache and main memory. In modern architectures, a cache line is usually 64 bytes long. By filling the caches per cache line, spatial locality can be exploited to improve performance. The mapping between the main memory and the cache is determined by several strategies, i.e., direct mapping, N-way set associative, and fully associative. With direct mapping, each entry (a cache line) in the memory can only be put in one place in the cache, which makes addressing faster. Under fully associative strategy, each entry can be put in any place, which offers fewer cache misses. The N-way associative strategy is a compromise between direct mapping and fully associative—it allows each entry in the memory to be in any of N places in the cache, which is called a cache set. N-way associative is often used in practice, and the mapping is deterministic in terms of cache sets.

In addition, most architectures usually adopt a least recently-used (LRU) replacement strategy to evict a cache line when there is not enough room. Such a scheme essentially utilizes temporal locality for enhancing performance. The latency to access cache is much shorter than the latency to access main memory. In order to gain good CPU performance, we have to guarantee high cache hit rate so that high-latency memory accesses are reduced. In designing an in-memory management system, it is important to exploit the properties of spatial and temporal locality of caches. For example, it would be faster to access memory sequentially than randomly, and it would also be better to keep a frequently-accessed object resident in the cache. The advantage of sequential memory access is reinforced by the prefetching strategies of modern CPUs.

1.4.3 SRAM: Static Random Access Memory

SRAM is a type of random-access memory (RAM) that uses latching circuitry (flip-flop) to store each bit. SRAM is volatile memory; data is lost when power is removed. The term static differentiates SRAM from DRAM (dynamic random-access memory) which must be periodically refreshed. SRAM is faster and more expensive than DRAM; it is typically used for the cache and internal registers of a CPU while DRAM is used for a computer's main memory.

SRAM may be integrated as RAM or cache memory in micro-controllers (usually from around 32 bytes up to 128 kilobytes), as the primary caches in powerful microprocessors, such as the x86 family, and many others (from 8 KB, up to many megabytes), to store the registers and parts of the state-machines used in some microprocessors (see register file), on application-specific ICs, or ASICs (usually in the order of kilobytes) and in Field Programmable Gate Array and Complex Programmable Logic Device

SRAM offers a simple data access model and does not require a refresh circuit. Performance and reliability are good and power consumption is low when idle. Since SRAM requires more transistors per bit to implement, it is less dense and more expensive than DRAM and also has a higher power consumption during read or write access. The power consumption of SRAM varies widely depending on how frequently it is accessed.

This memory technology is the closest to the CPU since its access time is the nearest to the CPU clock speed. It can achieve that performance since it does not need to be refreshed; unfortunately, it is an expensive technology as it uses from six to eight transistors per bit [3].

Many categories of industrial and scientific subsystems, automotive electronics, and similar embedded systems, contain SRAM which, in this context, may be referred to as ESRAM.Some amount (kilobytes or less) is also embedded in practically all modern appliances, toys, etc. that implement an electronic user interface. SRAM is also used in personal computers, workstations, routers and peripheral equipment: CPU register files, internal CPU caches and external burst mode SRAM caches, hard disk buffers, router buffers, etc. LCD screens and printers also normally employ SRAM to hold the image displayed (or to be printed).

1.4.4 DRAM: Dynamic Random Access Memory

This is also a semiconductor-based memory on which the bit value can be kept indefinitely as long as power is applied. The charge of a capacitor is used to store information in it, and then one transistor is used to access the charge; unfortunately, the capacitor needs a periodic refresh. DRAM uses a two-level decoding structure organization. This scheme allows the refreshing of entire rows as well as increases in performance that come from buffering the memory rows into an SRAM inside the chip [3].

DRAM can also have its independent clock become asynchronous to enable:

- Burst bit transfers without having to specify additional address bits.
- The faster DRAM version is called double data rate SDRAM or DDR SDRAM. The name means that the memory can transfer data on the falling and rising edge of the clock, effectively duplicating the amount of information that the chips can produce.

Additionally, to sustain the highest bandwidths possible, memory is cleverly organized to read and write from multiple memory banks, each bank having its SRAM row buffer.

Recently, DRAM becomes inexpensive and large enough to make an in-memory database viable.

1.4.5 Flash Memory

Flash memory [2] is a type of electrically erasable programmable read-only memory (EEPROM).

There are two main types of flash memory: NOR flash and NAND flash, which are named for the NOR and NAND logic gates. NOR and NAND flash use the same cell design, consisting of floating gate MOSFETs. They differ at the circuit level depending on whether the state of the bit line or word lines is pulled high or low. In NAND flash, the relationship between the bit line and the word lines resembles a NAND gate; in NOR flash, it resembles a NOR gate.

Flash memory was invented at Toshiba in 1980 and is based on EEPROM technology. Toshiba began marketing flash memory in 1987. EPROMs had to be erased completely before they could be rewritten. NAND flash memory, however, may be erased, written, and read in blocks (or pages), which generally are much smaller than the entire device. NOR flash memory allows a single machine word to be written – to an erased location – or read independently. A flash memory device typically consists of one or more flash memory chips (each holding many flash memory cells), along with a separate flash memory controller chip.

The NAND type is found mainly in memory cards, USB flash drives, solid-state drives (those produced since 2009), feature phones, smartphones, and similar products, for general storage and transfer of data. NAND or NOR flash memory is also often used to store configuration data in numerous digital products, a task previously made possible by EEPROM or battery-powered static RAM. A key disadvantage of flash memory is that it can endure only a relatively small number of write cycles in a specific block [2].

Flash memory is used in computers, PDAs, digital audio players, digital cameras, mobile phones, synthesizers, video games, scientific instrumentation, industrial robotics, and medical electronics. Flash memory has fast read access time, but it is not as fast as static RAM or ROM. In portable devices, it is preferred to hard disks because of its mechanical shock resistance.

1.4.6 NVM: Non Volatile Memory

The term Non-Volatile Memory (NVM) is used to address any memory device capable of retaining state in the absence of energy [22]. NVMs provide performance speeds comparable to those of today's DRAM (Dynamic Random Access Memory) and, like DRAM, may be accessed randomly with little performance penalties. Unlike DRAM, however, NVMs are persistent, which means they do not lose data across power cycles. In summary, NVM technologies combine the advantages of both memory (DRAM) and storage (HDDs - Hard Disk Drives, SSDs - Solid State Drives).

NVMs present many characteristics that make them substantially different from HDDs. Therefore, working with data storage in NVM may take the advantage of using different approaches and methods that systems designed to work with HDDs do not support. Moreover, since the advent of NAND flash memories, the use of NVM as a single layer of memory, merging today's concepts of main memory and back storage, has been proposed [22], aiming to replace the whole memory hierarchy as we know. Such change in the computer architecture would certainly represent a huge shift on software development as well, since most applications and operating systems are designed to store persistent data in the form of files in a secondary memory and to swap this data between layers of faster but volatile memories.

Even though all systems running in such an architecture would inevitably benefit from migrating from disk to NVM, one of the first places one might look at, when considering this hardware improvement, would be the database management system.

Although these recent NVM technologies have many characteristics in common, such as low latency, byte-addressability and non-volatility, they do have some key differences. These differences have direct impact over fundamental metrics, such as latency, density, endurance and even number of bits stored per cell.

Most commonly avaliable NVM technology include [22]:

• Flash memory.
• Magnetoresistive RAM.
• Spin-Torque Transfer RAM.
• Phase-Change Random Access Memory (PCRAM, PRAM or PCM).
• Resistive RAM (RRAM).

1.4.7 Magnetic Disks

Magnetic disks are a collection of hard platters covered with a ferromagnetic recording material. Disks are the largest capacity level; however, they are also the slowest technology.

Magnetic disks are organized as follows[4]:

• Each disk surface is divided into concentric circles called tracks.
• Each track is divided into sectors that contain information.
• Sectors typically store from 512 to 4096 bytes.

To read or write on them an electromagnetic coil called a head is placed on a moving arm just above the surface of the platters. The disk must execute the following three step process to access the data it contains:

• Seek: Move the arm to the proper track.
• Rotational latency: Wait for the desired sector to rotate under the head.
• Transfer time: Read the complete consecutive blocks desired.

Figure 1.4 shows a comparison between the different memory technologies discussed above. The main differences are their storage capacity and their access times to perform an input-output operation on a single bit.

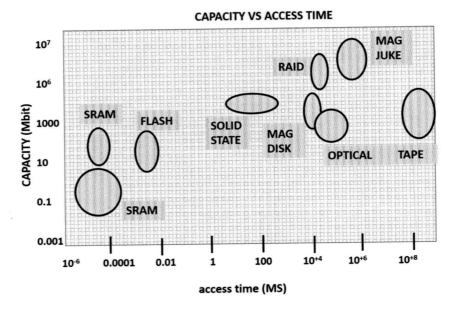

Fig. 1.4 Memory classes characterization

Even though memory becomes the new disk [21], the volatility of DRAM makes it a common case that disks are still needed to backup data. Data transmission between main memory and disks is conducted in units of pages, which makes use of data spatial locality on the one hand and minimizes the performance degradation caused by the highlatency of disk seek on the other hand. A page is usually a multiple of disk sectors which is the minimum transmission unit for hard disk. In modern architectures, OS usually keeps a buffer which is part of the main memory to make the communication between the memory and disk faster. The buffer is mainly used to bridge the performance gap between the CPU and the disk. It increases the disk I/O performance by buffering the writes to eliminate the costly disk seek time for every write operation, and buffering the reads for fast answer to subsequent reads to the same data. In a sense, the buffer is to the disk as the cache is to the memory. And it also exposes both spatial and temporal locality, which is an important factor in handling the disk I/O efficiently.

1.5 NUMA: Non-Uniform Memory Access

Non-uniform memory access is an architecture of the main memory subsystem where the latency of a memory operation depends on the relative location of the processor that is performing memory operations. Broadly, each processor in a NUMA system has a local memory that can be accessed with minimal latency, but can also access at least one remote memory with longer latency.

The main reason for employing NUMA architecture is to improve the main memory bandwidth and total memory size that can be deployed in a server node. NUMA allows the clustering of several memory controllers into a single server node, creating several memory domains. Although NUMA systems were deployed as early as 1980s in specialized systems [185], since 2008 all Intel and AMD processors incorporate one memory controller. Thus, most contemporary multi-processor systems are NUMA; therefore, NUMA-awareness is becoming a mainstream challenge.

In the context of data management systems, current research directions on NUMA-awareness can be broadly classified into three categories[21]:

- partitioning the data such that memory accesses to remote NUMA domains are minimized.
- managing NUMA effects on latency-sensitive workloads such as OLTP transactions.
- efficient data shuffling across NUMA domains.

Chapter 2
Memory Management

Memory management is part of the operating system responsible for the administration of memory. In this chapter we discuss several techniques to manage memory. This techniques vary from a primitive bare-machine approach to paging and segmentation techniques. Each approach has its own advantages and disadvantages. The selection of the most appropriate technique for memory management depends on many factors, especially on the hardware design of the system. As we shall discuss, many techniques require hardware support, although recent designs have closely integrated the hardware and operating system.

2.1 Background

In modern computer systems, the operating system resides in a part of main memory and the rest is used by multiple processes. The task of organizing the memory among different processes is called memory management. Memory management is a method in the operating system to manage operations in main memory and disk during process execution.

The operating system is responsible for the following activities in connection with memory management:

- Allocate and deallocate memory before and after process execution.
- To keep track of used memory space by processes.
- To minimize fragmentation issues.
- To achieve efficient and safe utilization of memory.
- To maintain data integrity while executing of process.

The selection of a memory-management strategy is a critical decision that needs to be addressed depending on the system. Some of these algorithms require hardware support and lead to a tightly integrated environment between the hardware and operating system memory management. Memory management is an important task that needs to be addressed by different parts of the computer system: hardware, operating system, services, and applications.

Each layer in the system, shown in Figure 2.1, provides a different set of services to the upper layer.

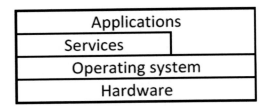

Fig. 2.1 Memory management stack

2.2 Address Binding

The Address binding process is the mechanism of associating entities from two different address spaces, mapping from one address space into another [7]. Computer systems store programs on disk as binary executable files. However, to be executed by a Von Neumann architecture processor, the program needs to be loaded into memory and placed within a process for the operating system to manage it properly. The processes on the disk are waiting for execution. When they are ready to execute, the operating system loads them into memory to a program and goes through several steps before executing. Addresses on the source program are generally symbolic. A compiler typically binds these symbolic addresses to relocatable addresses. The linker or loader finally turns the relocatable addresses to absolute addresses.

It is possible to bind instructions and data at any of the following steps:

- **Compile time**: If the compiler knows where the process will reside in memory, it can generate absolute code.
- **Load time**: The generation of relocatable code by the compiler delays binding until load time. If the starting address changes, the user code needs to be reloaded to reflect the change.
- **Execution time**: If the process can be moved during its execution from one memory segment to another, then the binding must be delayed until the runtime. Execution time binding requires specialized hardware.

2.3 Logical and Physical Address Space

As stated in chapter 1.2 above, the memory unit can safely ignore how any process generates the address given to the memory's input. However, proper memory management requires a distinction between logical and physical address space. An address generated by a CPU is referred to as a logical address, whereas a physical address refers to an address seen by the memory unit. Logical address is also called virtual address.

The compile-time and load-time address binding techniques generate the same logical and physical addresses. The execution time binding scheme, however, results in different logical and physical addresses [1]. Runtime mapping from a virtual to a physical address is done by a hardware device called a memory management unit (MMU) [7].

We can choose among different methods to accomplish such a mapping:

- Contiguous Memory Allocation.
- Paging.
- Segmentation.
- Segmentation with Paging.

Fig. 2.2 Address binding on the MMU

The concept of a logical address space that is bound to a separate physical address space is central to proper memory management. Figure 2.2 shows the process that an address produced by the central processing unit needs to undergo to reach the corresponding location in the memory. At the MMU there is a relocation register. The value on this register is added to every address generated by a user process at the time it is sent to memory. For example, if the base is at 15000, then an attempt by the user to address location 36 is dynamically relocated to location 15036.

The program of the user never accesses the physical addresses[1]. Only when it is used as a memory address (in an indirect load or store, perhaps) is it relocated relative to the relocation register. The user program deals with logical addresses. The memory mapping hardware converts logical addresses into physical addresses. The final location of a referenced memory address is not determined until the reference is made.

2.4 Dynamic Loading

If the computer system requires the entire program and data to be in physical memory for a process to execute, then the system has a hardware limit on the programs that can run on the system, since the size of a process must never exceed the size of physical memory. Dynamic loading can overcome this limitation, where the load time of a routine is the first time it is active. The operating system keeps all routines on disk in relocatable format; then when a program calls a routine, the calling routine first checks if the other routine is in memory. If not, the relocatable linking loader is called to load the desired routine into memory and to update the program's address tables to reflect the change. Finally, the newly loaded routine takes control of the system.

The advantage of dynamic loading is that a routine is loaded only when it is needed. This method is useful when large amounts of code are needed to handle infrequently occurring cases, such as error routines. In such a situation, although the total program size may be large, the portion that is used (and hence loaded) may be much smaller.

Dynamic loading does not require special support from the operating system. It is the responsibility of the users to design their programs to take advantage of such a method. Operating systems may help the programmer, however, by providing library routines to implement dynamic loading.

2.5 Dynamic Linking and Shared Libraries

Dynamically linked libraries (DLLs) are system libraries that are linked to user programs during execution [1]. Some operating systems support only static linking, in which system libraries are treated like any other object module and are combined by the loader into the binary program image. Dynamic linking, in contrast, is similar to dynamic loading. Here, linking is postponed until execution time. This feature is usually used with system libraries, such as the standard C language library. Without this facility, each program on a system must include a copy of its language library (or at least the routines referenced by the program) in the executable image. This requirement not only increases the size of an executable image but also may waste main memory. Another advantage of DLLs is that these libraries can be shared among multiple processes, so that only one instance of the DLL can be in main memory. For this reason, DLLs are also known as shared libraries, and are used extensively in Windows and Linux systems.

When a program references a routine that is in a dynamic library, the loader locates the DLL, loading it into memory if necessary. It then adjusts addresses that reference functions in the dynamic library to the location in memory where the DLL is stored.

DDLs can be extended to library updates (such as bug fixes). In addition, a library may be replaced by a new version, and all programs that reference the library will automatically use the new version. Without dynamic linking, all such programs would need to be relinked to gain access to the new library. So that programs will not accidentally execute new, incompatible versions of libraries, version information is included in both the program and the library. More than one version of a library may be loaded into memory, and each program uses its version information to decide which copy of the library to use. Versions with minor changes retain the same version number, whereas versions with major changes increment the number. Thus, only programs that are compiled with the new library version are affected by any incompatible changes incorporated in it. Other programs linked before the new library was installed will continue using the older library.

Unlike dynamic loading, dynamic linking and shared libraries generally require help from the operating system. If the processes in memory are protected from one another, then the operating system is the only entity that can check to see whether the needed routine is in another process's memory space or that can allow multiple processes to access the same memory addresses.

2.6 Swapping

Until this point in this chapter, a process needs to be in memory for execution. However, it can be swapped out of memory temporarily and brought back to memory for continued executing if it is not the only program running in the system. This technique allows the physical address space of all processes to exceed the real physical memory of the system. This technique is called swapping [1].

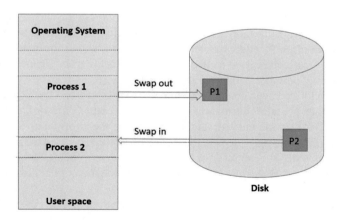

Fig. 2.3 Basic swapping mechanism

2.6.1 Standard Swapping

Standard swapping involves moving a process between main memory and a sufficiently large backing store. Figure 2.3 illustrates swapping.

The system maintains a ready queue consisting of all processes whose memory images are in the backing store or already in memory and are ready to run. Whenever the CPU scheduler decides to execute a process, it calls the dispatcher. The dispatcher checks whether the next process in the queue is in memory. If not and if there is no free memory region, the dispatcher swaps out a process currently in memory and swaps in the desired process. It then reloads the registers and transfers control to the process.

The context switch time in such a swapping system is relatively high. Modern operating systems do not use swapping since it requires too much time and provides too little execution time to be reasonable. Swapping is constrained by other factors as well. If we want to swap a process, we must be sure that it is completely idle. Of particular concern is any pending I/O.

2.7 Cache Management

Cache was the name given to represent the level of memory hierarchy between main memory and the processor in the first commercially available system with this extra level. The term is also used to refer to any management of storage using the locality principle for increased performance [7].

Two fundamental questions require an answer when using a cache: How do we know if an item is in the cache? How do we find the item in the cache? The simplest way to answer those questions is to assign a location in the cache for each word in memory based on its address, such as a simple hash structure without collision support [2]. This technique is called a direct mapped cache. Figure 2.4 shows a sample mapping of a direct mapped cache.

Since each location can contain multiple memory addresses, the cache requires a set of tags. Tags contain information that identify whether the word in the cache is the requested word in memory. A valid bit also marks the information in the cache as still valid. From a memory address, the low order bits can be used to find the unique cache entry to which the address could map. The index of the cache block, together with the tag contents of the block, uniquely identify the memory address of the word contained in the cache.

The total number of bits needed for a cache is a function of the cache and the address sizes because the cache includes both the storage for the data and the tags [2]. Larger blocks exploit spatial locality to lower miss rates. Increasing the block size usually decreases the miss rate. The miss rate will eventually increase if the block size becomes a significant fraction of the cache size. The increase happens because the cache is too small and the number of blocks it contains is too low. A susequent chapter explains this problem. Another problem with increasing the block size is

Cache	1	2	3	4	5	6	7	8	9
	10	11	12	13	14	15	16	17	18
	19	20	21	22	23	24	25	26	27
Main Memory	28	29	30	31	32	33	34	35	36
	37	38	39	40	41	42	43	44	45
	46	47	48	49	50	51	52	53	54
	55	56	57	58	59	60	61	62	63

Fig. 2.4 Direct mapped cache

that it also increases the time cost of a miss. This cost can be partially improved if the memory transfers are designed to be more efficient for big chunks of memory. A technique used for doing this is called early restart, where the process regains control just after the missing hit is already present in the cache, that way the process does not need to wait for the complete memory transfer.

2.7.1 Cache Misses

The control unit must detect a cache miss and process the miss by fetching the requested data from memory. If the cache reports a hit, the computer continues using the data as if nothing happened [7].

Processing a cache miss creates a pipeline stall instead of an interrupt that would require saving the state of all registers. More sophisticated out of order processors can allow instructions while waiting for cache misses. If an instruction access results in a miss, then the contents of the instruction register is invalid. To get the proper instruction into the cache, we must instruct the lower level of the memory hierarchy to perform a read.

The following steps must be taken by the hardware on a cache miss [2]:

1. Send the desired memory address to the memory.
2. Instruct the main memory to perform a read and wait for it to perform the access.
3. Write the cache entry, putting the data from memory into the data portion, write the upper part of the address to the tag field and set the valid bit.
4. Restart instruction execution cycle.

2.7.2 Writing into the Cache

Suppose on a store instruction we wrote the data only into the data cache, then after the write, the cache and the memory would have different values. They are said to be inconsistent [2]. One way to avoid this is to always write to cache and memory. This scheme is called write-through. This is straightforward, but it does not provide outstanding performance. To solve this, we could use a write buffer. The write buffer's responsibility is to wait for the data to reach memory. After the processor has written the data into the cache and the buffer, it can continue execution.

Another scheme is called write-back: When a write occurs, the new value is written only into the cache block, and the modified block is only written to the lower memory level when it is replaced [7]. Considering a miss, implementing stores efficiently in a cache that uses write back strategy is more complicated than in a write-through cache since the processor must first write the block back to memory if the data in the cache is modified, and then it can attend the cache miss. If the processor only overwrote the block, it would destroy the contents of the block, which is not backed up to the next lower level of the memory hierarchy. Write-back caches usually include write buffers that are used to reduce the miss penalty when a miss replaces a modified block.

2.7.3 Cache Associativity

At one extreme, there is the direct mapping technique which maps any block to a single location in the upper level of the memory hierarchy. At the opposite extreme is a scheme where any location in the cache can contain any given block. The name of this scheme is fully associative because any block in memory associates to any other entry in the cache. This scheme also means that to find a block in the cache the processor needs to search all the entries. The search is done in parallel using a comparator on hardware, which makes fully associative placement only viable on caches with a small number of blocks [2].

Another scheme is called set associative, where a block can belong only to a fixed number of locations. The cache divides into n sets. The advantage of increasing the level of associativity is that it usually decreases the miss rate. The choice between a direct-mapping, a set associative or a fully associative mapping in any memory hierarchy will depend on the cost of a miss versus the cost of implementing associativity both in time and in extra hardware and many other related factors [7].

2.7.4 Block Replacement

In the associative cache, we have a choice of where to place the requested block and hence a choice of which block to replace. The most commonly used scheme is least recently used (LRU). It keeps track of the usage history of each element set relative to the other elements in the set.

2.7.5 Multilevel Caches

Modern processors use multiple levels of cache to close the gap between fast clock rates and memory access times. The second level of caching is normally located on the same chip and is accessed whenever a miss occurs on the primary cache; figure 2.5 illustrates this.

If neither the primary nor the secondary cache contains the data, one memory access is required, and a more substantial miss penalty is incurred [7].

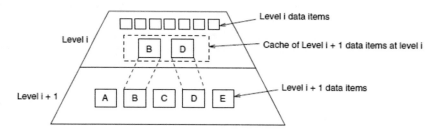

Fig. 2.5 Direct mapped cache

2.8 Contiguous Memory Allocation

Main memory must accommodate the operating system and user processes if different processes share the CPU in the system.

The operating system can be placed on either lower or higher memory. The only significant factor affecting the decision is the location of the interrupt vector since it is more comfortable if the operating system's memory map contains the interrupt vector. The operating system is usually on low memory, as well as the interrupt vector. In contiguous memory allocation, each process resides in a single section of memory that is contiguous to the section containing the next process [1]. This behavior is a particular instance of the general dynamic storage allocation problem, and there are two basic approaches for managing the continuous memory regions:

- Fixed partition scheme.
- Variable partition scheme.

In the fixed sized partitions scheme, each partition contains one process and:

- When a partition is free, a process is selected from the input queue and is loaded into the free partition.
- When a process terminates, its partition becomes free.

In the variable partition scheme, the operating system keeps a table indicating which parts of memory are available.

- Initially all memory is available. When a process starts, it loads into memory, and it can then compete for CPU time.
- At any given time, there is a list of available block sizes and an input queue. The operating system can order the input queue according to a scheduling algorithm.
- The memory blocks available comprise a set of holes of various sizes scattered throughout memory.
- When a process needs memory the system searches for a block that is large enough. If the hole is too large, then it is split into two: one for the process and the other for the set of available blocks. When a process terminates, it releases its block of memory, and it returns to the available blocks.
- When the operating system searches the available blocks to assign a memory block to a process it can take three basic approaches: first fit, best fit, worst fit.

2.9 Fragmentation

Operating systems usually allocate memory on multiples of a block size. The difference between the allocated size and the requested size is called internal fragmentation.

There is also external fragmentation, where there is enough total memory space to satisfy a request but the available spaces are not contiguous. First-fit and best fit suffer from external fragmentation [1]. A solution for external fragmentation is called compaction. This is not always possible,however. As an example, if relocation is static (done at assembly or load time), compaction cannot be done. If relocation is dynamic and delayed until execution time, compaction is possible. Another solution to external fragmentation is to permit the logical address space of the process to be non-contiguous.

2.10 Segmentation

Segmentation is a way to map the programmer's view of memory to the actual physical memory [7]. A logical address space is a collection of segments. Each segment has a name and a length. Addresses specify both the segment name and the offset within the segment. Figure 2.6 shows a representation of logical address space.

The programmer specifies each address by two quantities: a segment name and an offset. When using segmentation, objects are referred as two-dimensional addresses, but the actual memory is a one-dimensional array. To solve this problem a table called the segment table does mapping between the object space and the memory space. Each entry on the segment table contains the segment base and the segment limit, which represent the starting physical address and the size of the segment when the segment resides in memory [2].

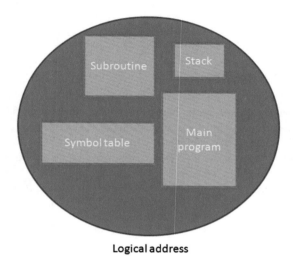

Fig. 2.6 Logical address

2.11 Paging

Paging is another memory management technique that allows physical address space to be non-contiguous. Therefore paging has the huge advantage of avoiding external fragmentation and the need for compaction.

When swapping out fragments to the backing store, the backing store also gets fragmented, but its access is much slower, making compaction impossible [1].

Paging involves breaking physical memory into fixed blocks called frames and breaking logical memory into blocks of the same size called pages. When a process loads, its pages load into any available memory frames before the process starts executing.

Every logical address divides into two parts: a page number and a page offset (as shown in Figure 2.7. The page table uses the page number as an index. The page table contains the base address of each page in physical memory. The hardware defines the page size, and it is a power of 2 [7].

Note that the size of memory in a paged system is different from the maximum logical size of a process.

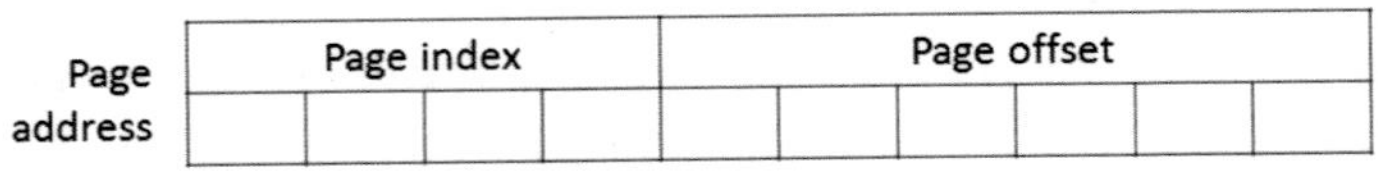

Page address	Page index				Page offset				

Fig. 2.7 Page address break down

2.11.1 Hardware Support

Most contemporary computers allow the page table to be huge (as many as 1 million entries). The memory contains the page table and a register points to the base of the page table. Unfortunately, this scheme slows memory access by a factor of two.

The standard solution to this problem is to use a specialized, small, and fast lookup hardware cache (or translation look-aside buffer, the TBL). The TBL takes as an input the page number from the logical address and compares it simultaneously against all keys.

- If the page number matches with a key, then its frame number is returned and immediately available to access memory.
- If the page number is not in the TBL, a memory reference to the page table must be made.
- If the TBL is already full of entries, an existing entry must be selected for replacement. Replacement policies range from least recently used, through round-robin to random.

The hit ratio refers to the percentage of times that the TBL contains the page number of interest [1].

2.11.2 Shared Memory

An advantage of paging is the possibility of sharing common code. This consideration is particularly important in a time-sharing environment.

A reentrant code is a non-self-modifying code. It never changes during execution so two or more processes can execute the same code at the same time.

Each process has its copy of registers and data to hold the data for process execution; however, the operating system needs to enforce the read-only nature of shared code [1].

2.12 Page Table Organization

Most modern computer systems support a significant, 64 bit, logical address space. In such an environment, the page table becomes excessively large. For this reason, it becomes unfeasible to allocate the page table contiguously in main memory.

2.12.1 Hierarchical Paging

One way to solve this problem is to use a two-level paging algorithm, in which the page table itself gets paged as well. This scheme is also known as a forward-mapped page table. The page number is further divided where p_1 is an index to the outer page table, and p_2 is the displacement within the page of the inner page table (Figure 2.8).

Page	Page index		Page offset
address	P_1	p^2	

Fig. 2.8 Hierarchical page address break down

The outer page table can also be paged, resulting in a three-level paging scheme (Figure 2.9). For 64 bit architectures, hierarchical page tables are considered inappropriate because of the increased number of accesses to memory [1].

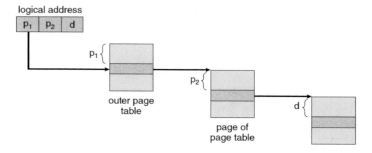

Fig. 2.9 2 Level hierarchical paging

2.12.2 Hashed Page Table

If we consider the page number to be the hashed value, each entry in the hashed table contains a linked list of frames that map to the same page number. Each element consists of the following three fields:

- P_1 page number
- P_2 page frame
- P_3 next node on the linked list.

The "clustered page tables" is a proposed variation of this in which each entry in the hash table refers to several pages rather than a single page [1].

2.12.3 Inverted Page Table

Inverted page tables are another way to solve this problem. There is exactly one entry for each frame of memory and each entry consists of the logical address of the page stored at exactly that physical address. Thus, just one single page table is in the system, and it has only one entry for each page of physical memory.

Unfortunately, the systems that use inverted page tables have more difficulties in implementing shared memory since shared memory is usually implemented using several logical addresses that map to one physical address. This technique cannot be used with inverted page tables because there is only one virtual page entry for every physical page [1].

2.13 Memory Protection

Another requirement that memory sharing introduces in the operating system is memory protection. For proper system operation, the Operating System must protect different processes from another. That is, the operating system area should only be accessible by the operating system, and each user process should only access its area. Hardware must provide this protection of the processor; otherwise, the operating system needs to interfere between the processor and each of its memory accesses [2].

There are different techniques that the operating system can use to implement memory protection. For example, to separate memory areas, we need the ability to identify a range of legal addresses for each process and ensure that each process only accesses its legal addresses.

This protection can be provided using two registers: base and limit [6]. The protection of a memory region requires the CPU hardware compare every address generated in user mode with these two registers. The operating system can only load the base and limit registers by using a privileged instruction that is only allowed to execute in kernel mode. This strategy also allows the operating system to have unrestricted access to process spaces and to load 2 or more processes on overlapping memory areas for debugging purposes [1].

2.13.1 Protection in Contiguous Memory Allocation

Since memory regions are contiguous, it is crucial for the operating system to ensure that a process can only access its memory. To accomplish this, when the scheduler selects a process for execution, the dispatcher loads the relocation and limit registers with the correct values as part of the context switch. Since relocation and limit registers are used to protect memory, this method protects the operating system and user processes from each other.

The relocation register scheme provides an effective way to allow the operating system's size to change dynamically. This register is particularly useful for device drivers. Such a code is a transient operating system code since it comes and goes as needed [1].

2.13.2 Protection in Paged Memory

In a paged environment each frame has a set of specially purposed protection-bits to accomplish memory protection. Normally these bits are kept in the page table. One bit can mean that the frame has read-write or read-only permissions. Since every reference to memory must pass through the page table to find its frame number, the protection bits can be verified to ensure that no invalid access is being intended [7].

There is one page table per running process and a different one for the operating system, so this scheme allows the operating system to have access to user processes page tables and pages as well as prevent a process from accessing the frames and page tables of a different process.

Chapter 3
Virtual Memory

In previous chapter we discussed several memory management techniques used in modern operating systems. All these tecniques share the same goal: to keep many processes in memory simultaneously to allow multiprogramming. However, they require the entire process to be in memory before the process can execute. Virtual memory is a technique that allows the execution of the processes that may not be completely in memory. One major advantage of this scheme is that processes can be larger than the available physical memory. This technique abstracts main memory into a very large , uniform array of storage, separating logical memory as viewed by the user from physical memory. This technique frees programmers from taking care of main memory limitations. Virtual memory also allows processes to share files and address spaces. Virtual memory is not easy to implement, however, and may substantially decrease preformance if it is used carelessly. In this chapter, we discuss virtual memory management.

3.1 Basic Concepts

The cache is a special fast memory buffer, typically within the CPU chip, used to increase access speed to main memory. We can apply the same technique to main memory and to secondary storage so that the main memory can act as a cache for the secondary storage (hard disks). This technique is called virtual memory. Unfortunately, virtual memory is not easy to implement and may substantially decrease performance if it is used carelessly [2]. There are various major motivations for virtual memory:

- Efficient and safe sharing of memory among multiple programs.
- Allows the execution of processes that are not completely in memory.
- Allows processes to share files and to implement shared memory easily.

© The Author(s), under exclusive license to Springer Nature Switzerland AG 2022
P. Mejia Alvarez et al., *Main Memory Management on Relational Database Systems*,
SpringerBriefs in Computer Science, https://doi.org/10.1007/978-3-031-13295-7_3

The ability to execute a program that is partially in memory offers the following advantages:

- A program would not be constrained to execute by the amount of physical memory.
- Increased concurrency since each program could take less physical memory; therefore more programs could fit in memory.
- Less I/O would be needed to load user programs into memory initially.
- In many cases, the entire program is not needed, for example:
    Code to handle unusual error conditions.
    Arrays, lists, and tables usually allocate more memory than they need.
    Rarely used features.
    The entire program might not be needed all at the same time.

The principle of locality enables virtual memory as well as caches. Virtual memory enables efficient sharing of the processor as well as of the main memory. For example:

- The behavior of multiple virtual machines sharing the memory changes dynamically. Because of this interaction, each program compiles into its address space a separate range of memory locations available only to this program. The virtual address space of a process refers to the logical view of how a process sees the memory.
- Virtual memory is responsible for implementing the translation of the program's virtual address space to the physical address space.
- This translation enforces protections of program's address space from other virtual machines.
- Virtual memory involves the separation of the logical memory address as perceived by the user from physical memory.

Although the concepts at work in virtual memory and caches are the same, their different historical roots have led to the use of different terminology. A page is the name of a virtual memory block. A virtual memory miss is called a page fault. With virtual memory, the processor produces a virtual address, which is translated by a combination of hardware and software into a physical address, which can then be used to access memory.

In virtual memory (shown in Figure 3.1), the address contains the virtual page number and a page offset. Having a larger number of virtual pages than physical pages is the basis for the illusion of an essentially unbounded amount of virtual memory [7]. Virtual memory also simplifies loading of the program for execution by providing relocation and enables a more straightforward implementation of shared libraries.

Relocation maps the virtual address used by the program to a different physical address before the address is used to access memory. It allows for loading the program anywhere in memory, instead of in a contiguous block.

Several processes can share system libraries through the mapping of the shared object into their virtual address space. Shared libraries enable a computer system to save space on disk and memory.

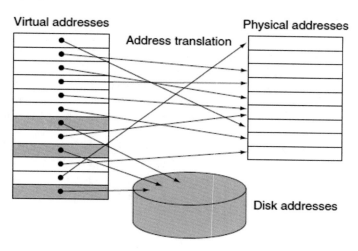

Fig. 3.1 Virtual memory representation

3.1.1 Page Access

The high cost of a page fault (millions of clock cycles) motivates many design choices in virtual memory. For example:

- Pages should be large enough to try to amortize high access time.
- Organizations that reduce the page fault rate are attractive, such as the fully associative placement of pages in memory.
- Page faults can be handled in software because overhead is small compared to disk access time.
- Write-through will not work since writes take way too long to complete. Virtual memory systems use write-back techniques.

The difficulty of using a fully associative placement lies in locating an entry, since it can be anywhere in the upper level of the hierarchy. A full search is impractical. Pages are located using a table that indexes the memory: the page table. The page table, together with the program counter and the register, specifies the state of a virtual machine. We often refer to that state as a process [2].

The virtual page address alone does not immediately tell us where the page is on disk. The system must keep track of the location on disk of each page in virtual address space. If a valid bit for a virtual page is off, a page fault occurs. Because the system does not know ahead of time when it will replace a page in memory, the operating system usually creates the space on flash memory or disk for all the pages of a process when it creates the process. This space is called the swap space. It also creates a data structure to record where the disk stores each virtual page [2].

3.1.2 The TLB: Translation Lookaside Buffer

Since main memory stores the page tables, every memory access by a program can take at least twice as long. Accordingly, modern processors include a unique cache that keeps track of recently used translations: a translation lookaside buffer (TLB). Because we access the TLB instead of the page table on every reference, the TLB will need to include other all status bits. The process followed by the TLB is described in Figure 3.2.

Designers have used a wide variety of associativity in TLBs. Some systems use small fully associative TLBs; other systems use large TLBs often with small associativity [2].

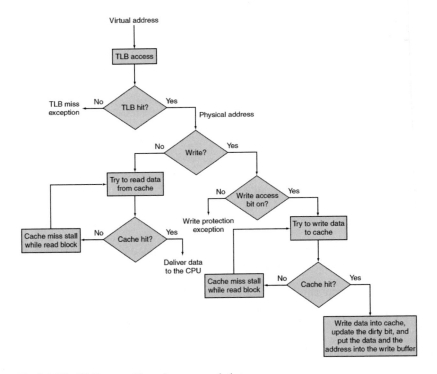

Fig. 3.2 The TLB page table and memory relation

3.1.3 Virtualization Challenges

I/O is the most complex part of the architecture to virtualize due to the increasing diversity of devices that can be attached to a system. Another challenge is the virtualization of virtual memory. For this to work the VMM separates the notion of real and physical memory:

- Real memory is a separate and intermediate level between virtual and physical memory.
- The guest OS maps virtual memory to real memory using its page tables.
- The VMM pages tables map the guest OS's real memory to physical memory.

3.2 Demand Paging

3.2.1 Basic Concepts

With demand-paged virtual memory, pages are loaded into frames in physical memory only when program execution demands this. Thus, not all the pages that are accessed are therefore never loaded into main memory. In some sense, a demand-paging system is similar to a paging system where processes reside in secondary memory. When the operating system swaps in a process, the pager guesses which pages it will use before the OS swaps out the process again, but instead of swapping in the whole process, the pager brings only those pages into memory.

This scheme requires some hardware support to distinguish between the pages that are in memory and the pages that are on disk. The page table often contains a valid-invalid bit for this reason [1]. As usual, the system sets the page table entry when a page loads into memory, but the one for a page that is not currently in memory is either marked invalid or contains the address of the page on disk. If the pager guesses right and pages in all the pages that are needed, the process will run correctly, as if it has all its pages in memory. Otherwise, if the process tries to access a page that the system did not load into memory, a page fault occurs. The paging hardware will notice the setting of the valid-invalid bit, causing a trap to the operating system [7].

The operating system will handle the page fault as follows.

1. Check whether the memory access qualifies as being valid or invalid.
2. If the reference is invalid, terminate the process.
3. Find a free frame.
4. Read the desired frame from disk to the available frame.
5. Modify the page table to indicate that the page is now in memory.
6. Restart the instruction that was interrupted by the trap.

A pure-demand paging system would not bring pages into memory until program execution needs them. However, this would result in unacceptable system performance.

The hardware support needed for demand paging is: Paging table and Secondary memory.

Paging is added between the CPU and the memory in a computer system and should be transparent for the user process. People often assume that any system can use paging. The assumption is only correct for non-demand-paging environments where a page fault represents a fatal error, and no instructions would require a restart operation.

3.2.2 Performance Considerations

Demand paging can significantly affect the performance of a computer system because the effective access time is directly proportional to the page fault rate. Disk IO to swap is generally faster than the file system. It is faster because swap space allocates much larger blocks and it does not use file lookups or indirect allocation methods.

Mobile operating systems typically do not support swapping. Instead, these systems demand-page from the file system and reclaim read-only pages from applications if memory becomes constrained.

3.3 Page Replacement

If we increase the degree of multiprogramming beyond the system's available memory, we are over allocating memory. If the system is over allocating more memory than a certain threshold, the following can occur:

- Page faults can occur while a user's process is executing.
- The operating system, therefore, determines that the desired page resides on disk and realizes that there are no free frames on the free-frame list.

In this case, the operating system has two main options:

- Terminate the user process.
- Swap out a different process, to release all its frames and to reduce the level of multiprogramming.

It is easy to expect that giving more memory to a process would improve its performance. This however, is not always the case: When an algorithm does not show the property, it is said to suffer from the Belady's anomaly, and it is undesirable [1].

3.3.1 Basic Page Replacement

Page replacement is essential to the demand paging scheme. It completes the separation between logical memory and physical memory. In general, page replacement takes the following approach:

1. Find the location of the desired page on disk.
2. Find a free frame.
   If there is a free frame, use it.
   If there is no free frame, use a page-replacement algorithm to select a victim frame.
   Write the victim frame to the disk: change the page and frame table accordingly.
3. Read the desired page into the newly freed frame, change the page and frame tables.
4. Continue the process from where the page fault occurred.

Notice that if there are no free frames, two-page transfers are required. The pages table contains a bit to indicate modifications to reduce overhead. The hardware sets the modify bit for a page whenever any byte in the page changes in memory [7].
When the system selects a page for replacement, it examines the modify bit.

- The system knows that the page contains differences between the version in memory and on disk when the bit is on. Therefore the system must write the page to disk.
- If the modify bit is off, the page has not been modified since it was read into memory so we can save one memory access.

The paging system designer must solve two major problems to implement demand paging:

- The system must decide how many frames to allocate to each process: this is known as a frame allocation algorithm.
- The system must choose the frames for replacement when it is required: a page replacement algorithm.

3.3.2 FIFO and Optimal Page Replacement

The simplest page replacement algorithm is a first-in, first-out (FIFO) algorithm. It associates each page with the time when that page loaded into memory. The system uses the timestamp to choose the oldest page for replacement. FIFO page replacement algorithm performance is not always right: If we select a page that is in active use by the executing process, the replacement algorithm will select some other page for replacement, and a new fault occurs almost immediately.

A lousy replacement decision increases the page fault rate and slows process execution; however, it does not cause incorrect execution [1].

Optimal page replacement requires future knowledge. However, if available it provides the lowest possible page fault rate for a fixed number of times. The main idea of OPT or MIN algorithms is to replace the page that the process will not use for the longest period [1].

3.3.3 LRU Page Replacement

If we use the recent past to get an approximation of the near future, then we can replace the page that the process has not used for the longest period. LRU replacement associates each page with the time of the page's last use. When the system selects a page for replacement, LRU chooses the page unused for the most extended period. LRU then becomes an approximation to the OPT page replacement strategy [7]. LRU usually requires substantial hardware assistance. Two possible implementations are:

- Counters: Associate each page table entry a time-of-use field and add a logical clock to the CPU.
  The clock is incremented for every memory reference.
  Whenever the process references a page, the hardware copies the clock register to the time-of-use field in the page table entry for that page.
  The page is replaced with the smallest time value. To accomplish this, it requires a search of the page table the LRU page and a write to memory for each memory access.
- Stack: Keep a stack of page numbers, and whenever the process references a page, its entry gets to the top of the stack.
  The top of the stack will always have the most recently used page, and the LRU page will always be at the bottom of the stack. Both 'counters' and 'stack' implementations of LRU require hardware assistance beyond TLB registers [1].

LRU like optimal replacement belongs to a set of page replacement algorithms called stack algorithms. All stack algorithms share the following characteristics:

- The set of pages in memory for N frames is always a subset of the set of pages that would be in memory with N+1 frames.
- Stack algorithms do not exhibit Belady's anomaly.

3.3.4 LRU Approximation Page Replacement

Few computer systems provide sufficient hardware support for true LRU page replacement. However, many systems provide a reference bit, which is set by the hardware, whenever a page is referenced [1]. Although it does not tell the order of use, many page replacement algorithms use the reference bit. These algorithms approximate LRU because of the following:

- Each entry in the page table has its reference bits.
- During program startup time the bits are cleared by the operating system.
- Whenever the process references a page, the bit is set by the hardware.

To implement LRU with the reference bit, the following is required:

1. Keep a byte for each page in a table in memory.
2. At regular intervals, the operating system shifts the reference bit for each page into the high-order bit of the byte, shifting the other bits to the right.

The register then contains the history of the pages used for the latest periods. If we interpret the byte as unsigned integers, the page with the lowest number is the LRU page and can be replaced [1].

3.3.4.1 Second Chance Algorithm

The second chance algorithm is a FIFO replacement algorithm. When it selects a page for replacement, it inspects its reference bit.

- If the page bit is off the page is replaced.
- If the page bit is on the page gets a second chance, and the next FIFO page on the LRU list is selected.

When a page gets a second chance, the system sets off its reference bit, and it restarts its arrival time to the current time. Therefore, when a page gets a second chance, it will not be replaced until all other pages have been replaced or given second chances [7].

3.3.4.2 Enhanced Second Chance Algorithm

This algorithm takes into account the number of I/O required to replace a page [1]. The enhanced second chance algorithm considers the reference bit and the modify bit to give a second chance to a page. It constructs using the table 3.3:

Reference	Modify	Description
0	0	Neither used nor modified: best page to replace.
0	1	Not recently used but modified: The page needs to be rewritten out before replacement.
1	0	Recently used but clean: Could be used again soon, but can be overwritten.
1	1	Recently used and modified: Worst page to replace

Fig. 3.3 Enhanced second chance posibilities

3.3.5 Counting Based Page Replacement

Counting based page replacement keeps a counter of the number of references that each page has. The algorithm can use any of the following two schemes:

- Least frequently used (LFU). The page with the smallest count is replaced.
- Most frequently used (MFU). The page with the smallest count was probably just brought in memory and has yet to be used.

This algorithm reports good performance for sequential file reads such as data warehouses [1].

3.3.6 Page Buffering

In addition to page replacement algorithms, the system can use page buffering. This consists of having a pool of free frames. The free frames pool is then used to increase system performance in the following scenarios [7]:

- At page fault time, a victim frame is selected for replacement by a newly required frame; however, the new frame is read into a free frame from the pool before the victim is written out.
- Finally, when the victim frame has finished being written out, its frame is moved into the free frames pool.

3.3.7 Applications and Page Replacement

Some applications perform worse when accessing data through the operating system's virtual memory system than if the operating system provided no buffering at all. A typical example of this is a database that provides its memory management and I/O buffering. Operating systems provide 'raw disk' which allows programs to use a disk partition as a sizable sequential array of logical blocks, without any file system structure to address this [1].

3.4 Allocation of Frames

If we now consider that a computer system can handle multiple processes running concurrently, we need to answer the following question: How do we allocate the fixed amount of free memory among various processes? [7]

One reason for allocating at least a minimum number of frames involves performance:

- As the number of frames allocated to each process decreases, the page fault rate increases, slowing process execution.
- A process must have enough frames to hold all the different stages that any instruction can reference during the complete instruction execution cycle. Otherwise, the instruction execution needs to restart.

The amount of available physical memory defines the maximum number of frames [1].

3.4.1 Allocation Algorithms

The easiest way to split M frames among N process is to give everyone an equal share MxN frames. The leftover frames can form a buffer of free frames. This technique is called equal allocation. Another option is proportional allocation where the available memory allocated to each process depends on the process's size. Therefore, all process share the available frames according to their needs. Some drawbacks of equal and proportional allocation are:

- The allocation may vary according to the multiprogramming level. When the operating system creates a new process, each existing process will lose some frames to provide the memory needed for the new process.
- There is no prioritization of processes. A high priority process gets the same treatment as a low priority process.

Proportional allocation could consider the program size and the process priority to follow process priorities [1].

3.4.2 Allocation Scope

Global page replacement allows a process to select a replacement frame from the set of all frames, even if a different process gets that frame. Global page replacement means that one process can take frames from another one. Alternately, local page replacement requires each process to select from its set of allocated frames only.

An allocation scheme where a process can select a replacement from among its frames and the frames of any lower priority process is also possible.

With global page replacement, a process may happen to select only frames allocated to other processes, thus increasing the number of frames allocated to it. One problem with global page replacement is that a process cannot control its page-fault rate, meaning that the same process can perform quite differently according to the multiprogramming level. Global replacement generally results in higher system throughput and is, therefore, the more commonly used method [1].

3.4.3 Non Uniform Memory Access considerations

In systems with multiple CPUs, a given CPU can access some sections of main memory faster than it can access others. These performance differences are caused by how CPUs and memory are physically wired and interconnected. NUMA systems are slower than systems in which memory and CPU colocate on the same motherboard. In NUMA systems, optimally locating page frames can significantly affect performance. The same type of exceptional management is also required on the scheduling system to get a well behaved NUMA system. The required managing changes consist of tracking the last CPU on which each process ran. The historical information is used by the scheduler to schedule each process onto its previous CPU. Then the memory management system allocates frames that are the closest to the CPU on which the process will be executing. This strategy improves cache hits and decreases memory access times in the system [1].

Solaris OS solves the problem by creating lgroups (locality groups) in the kernel. Each lgroup keeps together close CPUs and memory. It creates a hierarchy of lgroups based on the latency between them. Solaris tries to schedule all threads of a process and to allocate all the memory from a process within its lgroup. If it is not possible, it uses the closest lgroup using the hierarchy [10].

3.5 Memory Protection on Virtual Memory

The TBL or translation lookaside buffer is a special purpose cache on the processor used to speed up accesses to the page table in virtual memory.

The TBL plays an essential role in memory protection for virtual memory. To accomplish this when the operating system decides to change from running process P1 to running process P2, if there is no TLB loaded into the processor's cache, it is sufficient to change the page table register to point to P2's page table (rather P1's). However, if a TLB is already loaded, then all entries from P1 need to be cleared. A different common alternative to memory protection is to extend the virtual address space by adding a process identifier or task identifier into the address [2].

3.6 Thrashing

When a process has high paging activity, the CPU spends most of its time in juggling pages between the main memory and the swap device. This situation is called thrashing. When a severe thrashing scenario occurs, a process could be spending more time paging than executing.

Thrashing results in severe performance degradation and the system responsiveness may collapse. The operating system needs to prevent thrashing at all costs [7]. When the number of frames allocated to a low-priority process falls below the minimum required by the computer architecture, the operating system must suspend the low-priority process, then the process gets paged out, and its frames can be released.

The operating system monitors CPU optimization as a way to control the level of multiprogramming. If the CPU is underutilized, the scheduler can increase the level of multiprogramming. If global page replacement is being used at process creation time, frames are taken from other processes when it starts page faulting. The process needs those pages, so it also faults.

As the processes queue up on the paging device, the ready queue empties and CPU utilization decreases. The CPU scheduler sees the decreasing CPU utilization and increases the degree of multiprogramming again. At this point, to increase CPU utilization and stop thrashing, the operating system must decrease the degree of multiprogramming. Unfortunately, the CPU scheduler has done the opposite.

Using local page replacement or priority replacement, the effects of thrashing can be limited only. To prevent thrashing, approaches like the locality model of process execution must be used [1]. A locality is a set of pages that are active together, and the locality model states that, as a process executes, it moves from one locality to another. Therefore, a program is generally composed of several different localities. The program structure and its data structures define localities. The locality model states that all programs will exhibit this basic memory reference structure [7].

3.6.1 The Working Set Model

This model uses a parameter delta to define the working set window. Calculating the working set is hard [1].

- If a page is active in the process execution, the page will be in the working set. When the page is not active anymore, the working set will drop the page after n time units of its last reference.
- The working set is an approximation of the program's locality.
- The most important property of the working set is its size, which can vary over time.
- The demand of the computer memory system is the sum of the working set sizes of every process.
- If the demand is greater than the number of available frames, then thrashing will occur.

The operating system monitors the working set of each process. If there are enough extra frames, another process can start. If the demand of the system exceeds the total number of available frames, the operating system selects a process to suspend. The working set model is successful but is a somewhat clumsy way to control thrashing [7].

3.6.2 Page Fault Frequency

One of the properties of thrashing has a high page-fault rate. When the page fault is too high for a process, we know that it needs more frames. If it is too low, the process might have too many frames. The operating system can establish upper and lower bounds for page fault rate.

- The process gets a new frame if it exceeds the upper bound.
- The process loses a frame if it exceeds the lower bound.

If the page fault rate exceeds the upper bound and there are no available frames, the operating system can suspend a process and distribute the just released frames among the processes with high page fault rate.

3.7 A Common Framework for Managing Memory

In this section, we will discuss the common operational alternatives for memory management, and how these determine their behavior. We will examine these policies as a series of activities that apply between any two levels of a memory hierarchy, although for simplicity we will primarily use terminology for caches.

The activities mentioned are the following:

- Block Placement.
- Block Access.
- Block Replacement in Cache Miss.
- Parallelism and Memory Hierarchy.

3.7.1 Block Placement

The advantage of increasing the degree of associativity is that it is a way to control the miss rate and make it decrease. Improvement comes from reducing misses that compete for the same location. Some techniques for block placement are shown in Figure 3.4.

Scheme	Number of sets	Blocks per set
Direct mapped	Number of blocks in the cache	1
Set associative	(number of blocks in the cache)/associativity	Associativity (2-16 typically)
Fully associative	1	Number of blocks in the cache

Fig. 3.4 Block placement strategies

3.7.2 Block Access

The choice among direct-mapped, set-associativity or fully associative mapping in any memory hierarchy will depend on the cost of a miss versus the cost of implementing associativity, both in time and in extra hardware. Fully associative caches are generally prohibitive except for small sizes. For virtual memory, however, fully associative is used since misses are costly and sophisticated replacement schemes to reduce miss rates exist. Some techniques for block access are shown in Figure 3.5.

Associativity	Location method	Comparisons required
Direct mapped	Index	1
Set Associative	Index the set, search among elements	Degree of associativity
Fully associative	Search all cache entries	Size of the cache
Fully associative	Separate lookup table	0

Fig. 3.5 Block access strategies

3.7.3 Block Replacement in Cache Miss

There are two primary strategies for replacement in associative caches: random and LRU. For some workloads, random replacement can be better than LRU. In caches, the replacement algorithm is a hardware module, which means that the scheme should be easy to implement. In virtual memory, however, the system performs a LRU approximation.

Cache misses can fall into the following categories according to their nature [2]:

- Compulsory misses: These are cache misses caused by the first access to a block that has never been in the cache (cold start).
- Capacity misses: Caused when the cache cannot contain all the blocks needed during the execution of the program.
- Conflict misses: When multiple blocks compete for the same set (collision misses).

3.7.4 Parallelism and Memory Hierarchy

Multicore multiprocessor means multiple processors on a single chip. These processors very likely share a common physical address space, which means they share data.

Caching shared data introduces a new problem because the view of memory held by individual processors is through their caches. This behavior is known as the cache coherence problem. Coherence defines the values that a read operation can return. Consistency determines when a read will return a written value. A memory system is coherent if it shows the following characteristics:

- A read by processor P to a location X that follows a write by P to X, with no other writes of X by a different processor between the write and the read, always returns the value written by P.
- A read by a processor to location X that follows a write by another processor to X returns the written value if the read and write have enough separation in time, and no other writes to X occur between the two accesses.
- Writes to the same location are serialized: Two writes to the same location by any two processors are seen in the same order by all processors.

The first property preserves program order and the second property defines the notion of what it means to have a coherent view of memory [2].

3.7.4.1 Basic Coherence Enforcement

In a coherent cache multiprocessor, caches provide both migration and replication of shared data items:

- Migration: A data item can be moved to a local cache and used there transparently. Migration reduces latency and bandwidth demand on the shared memory to access shared data items that come from a remote allocation.
- Replication: While simultaneously reading shared data, caches make a copy of the data item in the local cache. Replication reduces both latency of access and contention for a read shared data item.

The protocols to maintain coherence for multiple processors are called cache coherence protocols. Key to implementing a cache coherence protocol is tracking the state of any sharing data of a data block [2].

3.7.4.2 Snooping Protocols

One method of enforcing coherence is to ensure that a processor has exclusive access to a data before it writes that item. This style of protocols is called a write invalidate protocol because it invalidates copies in other caches on a write.

Consider one write access followed by one read access by another processor: since the write requires exclusive access, any copy held by the reading processors must be invalidated, and the cache is forced to fetch a new copy of the data. One insight is that block size plays an essential role in cache coherency since most protocols exchange full blocks between processors, thereby increasing coherency bandwidth demands. Large blocks can cause what is called false sharing: when the same cache block contains two independent shared variables, the full block is exchanged between processors even though the processors are accessing different variables. False sharing should be considered at the programming time and during the compilation process.

In addition to the snooping cache coherence protocol, where it distributes the status of the shared blocks, a directory-based cache coherence protocol keeps the sharing status of the block of physical memory in just one location called the directory.

Directory-based cache coherence protocols have slightly higher implementation overhead than snooping but they can reduce traffic between caches and thus scale to larger processor counts [2].

3.8 Other Considerations

The selection of a replacement algorithm and memory allocation policy are the major decision that we make for a paging policy. However, in this section we will discuss otehr considerations as well.

3.8.1 Pre-Paging

Pre-paging is an attempt to prevent a high level of initial paging. The strategy is to bring all the needed pages into memory at one time. In a system using the working set model, the operating system stores a list of the pages in the working set when it suspends the process, and it brings them all back together when the process can be resumed [1].

3.8.2 Page Size

While building a new CPU, the designer can consider the page size to use. Page sizes are invariably a power of two. There is, however, a set of factors that support various page sizes:

- Page table size: For a fixed virtual memory space, decreasing the page size increases the number of pages and the size of the page table.
- Since each process needs a page table, a big page size is desirable.
- Memory is better utilized using smaller page sizes due to reduced internal fragmentation.
- Smaller page sizes reduce the number of I/O because better memory granularity achieves better program locality.
- A big page size decreases the number of page faults.

3.8.3 TLB Reach

The hit ratio for a TLB refers to the percentage of virtual address translations that are resolved in the TLB rather than on the page table. A way to increase the hit ratio is to increase the number of entries in the TLB; this is expensive, however. TLB reach refers to the amount of memory that is accessible from the TLB and is the number of entries multiplied by the page size. Doubling the number of TLB entries also doubles the TLB reach. If the page size can increase, then the TLB reach also increases. Applications like databases take advantage of huge pages. To increase page size, the TLB needs to be managed by software instead of hardware which is costly; however, the cost is often surpassed by the performance gains that come from the increased TLB hit ratio [1].

3.8.4 Inverted Page Table

Inverted page table management needs to store information about frames to pages into a separate page. This separate page is just another regular page. The purpose of this form of page management is to reduce the amount of physical memory needed to track virtual-to-physical address translations. Unfortunately, a page fault may cause the virtual memory manager to generate an additional page fault [1].

3.8.5 Program Structure

Demand paging is designed to be transparent to the user; however, system performance can be greatly improved if the user has an awareness of the underlying demand paging.

Careful selection of data structures can increase the locality and hence lower the page fault rate and the number of pages in the working set.

- Stack data structures have good locality since accesses are only made to the top.
- Hashes data structures have bad locality since they are designed to scatter references.

Locality is yet another measurement of the efficiency of a data structure.

The compiler and loader can have a significant effect on paging. Separating the code and data and generating reentrant code means that code pages can be read-only and hence will never be modified. The loader and related routines can fit on the same page. This strategy is an instantiation of the bin-packing problem of operations research [1].

3.8.6 Page Locking

When a system uses demand paging, it sometimes needs to allow some of the pages to be locked in memory. For this reason, every frame has its lock bits. If the frame is locked, it is not susceptible to page replacement. Various situations can take advantage of lock bits:

- Some parts of the operating systems need to be locked into memory (the memory manager for example).
- A database may want to manage a chunk of memory.

Pinning or locking of memory is common, and most operating systems have a system call allowing an application to pin some region of its address space. Unfortunately, it can cause stress to the memory management algorithm. Locking memory can also be dangerous; the lock bit can be set and never reset. If that situation ever happens, then the locked frame becomes unusable [1].

3.8.7 Memory Mapped Files

Memory mapping a file allows a part of the virtual address space to be logically associated with a file to enable performance benefits. Memory mapping a file is accomplished by mapping a disk block to a page in memory (Figure 3.6). Initial access to the file proceeds through normal demand paging, resulting in a page fault, however, a page-sized portion of the file is read from the file system onto a physical page. Writes to the file mapped in memory are not necessarily synchronous writes to the file on disk. When a process closes the file, all the memory-mapped data is written back to disk and removed from the virtual memory of the process. Multiple processes may be allowed to map the same file concurrently to allow sharing data.

Memory-mapping system calls can also support copy on write functionality, allowing processes to share a file in read-only mode but to have their copies of the data they modify.

Shared memory is often implemented using memory mapping of a file [1].

Each I/O controller includes registers to hold commands and data to be transferred. Many computer architectures provide memory-mapped I/O to allow more convenient access to I/O devices. Ranges of memory addresses are set aside and mapped to the device registers. Reads and writes to these memory addresses cause the data to be transferred to and from the device registers [1].

3.8.8 Kernel Memory Allocation

When a process running in user mode requests additional memory, the operating system allocates pages from the list of free page frames maintained by the kernel.

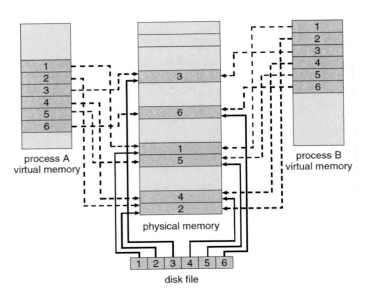

Fig. 3.6 Memory mapped file

The kernel itself allocates memory from a free-memory pool different from the list used to satisfy conventional user-mode processes for the following reasons:

- To minimize waste due to fragmentation. This optimization is especially important since the operating system does not page its code or data.
- Pages allocated for user-mode processes do not necessarily have to be a contiguous physical memory area; however, certain hardware devices may require memory residing in physically contiguous pages.

3.8.8.1 Buddy System

The buddy system allocates memory from a fixed-size segment consisting of physically contiguous pages. Memory is allocated from this segment using a power of 2 allocators.

An advantage of the buddy system is that adjacent buddies can be merged to form larger segments using a technique called coalescing. The drawback to the buddy system is that rounding to the highest power of 2 is very likely to cause fragmentation within allocated segments. It cannot guarantee that less than 50% of the allocation unit will be wasted due to internal fragmentation [1].

3.8.8.2 Slab Allocation

A slab is made up of one or more physically contiguous pages, and a cache consists of one or more slabs (Figure 3.7). Each unique kernel data structure has its cache. Each cache populates with an object that is an instantiation of the kernel data structures associated with the cache. The slab allocation algorithm uses caches to store kernel objects. When the operating system creates a cache, It preallocates some free objects into the cache. When a new object for a kernel data structure is needed, the allocator can assign any free object from the cache and marks it as used [11].

The slab allocator provides two main benefits:

- No memory is wasted due to fragmentation.
- Memory can be assigned very quickly. This behavior is particularly effective for managing memory when creation and destruction of objects are frequent.

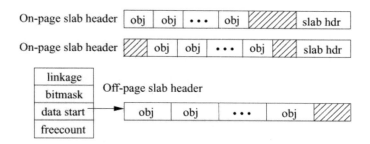

Fig. 3.7 Slab allocator data structure

3.8.9 Virtual Machines

The broadest definition of a VM includes all emulation methods that provide standard software interface, such as the Java VM. VMs provide at least two benefits that are commercially significant:

- Managing software: An abstraction to run a complete software stack.
- Managing hardware: A complete software stack can run on independent servers that share hardware.

The cost of processor virtualization depends on the workload.

- User level processor-bound programs have no virtualization overhead.
- OS intensive programs have great virtualization overhead.

The qualitative requirements for a virtual machine monitor (VMM) are:

- The guest software should behave on an MV exactly as in native hardware.
- The guest software should not be able to change the allocation of real system resources directly.

Because the VMM must ensure that the guest system only interacts with virtual resources, a conventional guest runs as a user-mode program on top of the VMM. Then if a guest OS attempts to use a privileged instruction, it will trap to the VMM, which can then affect the appropriate action on the real resources.

In the absence of this support, a VMM must take special precautions to locate all problematic instructions, increasing the complexity of the VMM and reducing the performance of the guest software [2].

3.9 Hardware Memory Management Real Examples

3.9.1 Memory Management in the IA-32 Architecture

The memory management facilities of the IA-32 architecture are divided into two parts [49]: segmentation and paging. Segmentation provides a mechanism of isolating individual code, data, and stack modules so that multiple programs (or tasks) can run on the same processor without interfering with one another. Paging provides a mechanism for implementing a conventional demand-paged, virtual-memory system where sections of a program's execution environment are mapped into physical memory as needed. Paging can also be used to provide isolation between multiple tasks. When operating in protected mode, some form of segmentation must be used. There is no mode bit to disable segmentation. The use of paging, however, is optional.

These two mechanisms (segmentation and paging) can be configured to support simple single-program (or singletask) systems, multitasking systems, or multiple-processor systems that used shared memory. As shown in Figure 3.8[49], segmentation provides a mechanism for dividing the processor's addressable memory space (called the linear address space) into smaller protected address spaces called segments. Segments can be used to hold the code, data, and stack for a program or to hold system data structures (such as a TSS or LDT). If more than one program (or task) is running on a processor, each program can be assigned its own set of segments. The processor then enforces the boundaries between these segments and insures that one program does not interfere with the execution of another program by writing into the other program's segments. The segmentation mechanism also allows typing of segments so that the operations that may be performed on a particular type of segment can be restricted.

All the segments in a system are contained in the processor's linear address space. To locate a byte in a particular segment, a logical address (also called a far pointer) must be provided. A logical address consists of a segment selector and an offset. The segment selector is a unique identifier for a segment. Among other things it provides an offset into a descriptor table (such as the global descriptor table, GDT) to a data

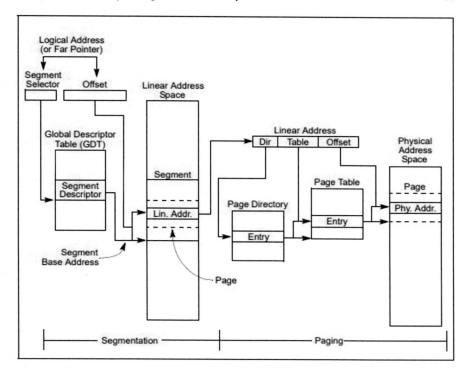

Fig. 3.8 IA-32 Segmentation and Paging

structure called a segment descriptor. Each segment has a segment descriptor, which specifies the size of the segment, the access rights and privilege level for the segment, the segment type, and the location of the first byte of the segment in the linear address space (called the base address of the segment). The offset part of the logical address is added to the base address for the segment to locate a byte within the segment. The base address plus the offset thus forms a linear address in the processor's linear address space.

If paging is not used, the linear address space of the processor is mapped directly into the physical address space of processor. The physical address space is defined as the range of addresses that the processor can generate on its address bus.

Because multitasking computing systems commonly define a linear address space much larger than it is economically feasible to contain all at once in physical memory, some method of "virtualizing" the linear address space is needed. This virtualization of the linear address space is handled through the processor's paging mechanism.

Paging supports a "virtual memory" environment where a large linear address space is simulated with a small amount of physical memory (RAM and ROM) and some disk storage. When using paging, each segment is divided into pages (typically 4 KBytes each in size), which are stored either in physical memory or on the disk. The operating system or executive maintains a page directory and a set of page tables to keep track of the pages. When a program (or task) attempts to access an address location in the linear address space, the processor uses the page directory and page tables to translate the linear address into a physical address and then performs the requested operation (read or write) on the memory location.

If the page being accessed is not currently in physical memory, the processor interrupts execution of the program (by generating a page-fault exception). The operating system or executive then reads the page into physical memory from the disk and continues executing the program.

When paging is implemented properly in the operating-system or executive, the swapping of pages between physical memory and the disk is transparent to the correct execution of a program. Even programs written for 16-bit IA32 processors can be paged (transparently) when they are run in virtual-8086 mode.

3.9.2 Memory Management in the AMD64 Architecture

by The AMD64 Architecture uses segmentation and/or paging memory management methods. Usually, memory management is not visible to application software. It is handled by the system software and processor hardware.

3.9.2.1 AMD64 Segmentation

The AMD64 architecture [50] is designed to support all forms of legacy segmentation. However, most modern system software does not use the segmentation features available in the legacy x86 architecture. Instead, system software typically handles program and data isolation using page-level protection. For this reason, the AMD64 architecture dispenses with multiple segments in 64-bit mode and, instead, uses a flat-memory model. The elimination of segmentation allows new 64-bit system software to be coded more simply, and it supports more efficient management of multi-processing than is possible in the legacy x86 architecture.

Segmentation is, however, used in compatibility mode and legacy mode. Here, segmentation is a form of base memory-addressing that allows software and data to be relocated in virtual-address space off of an arbitrary base address. Software and data can be relocated in virtual-address space using one or more variable-sized memory segments. The legacy x86 architecture provides several methods of restricting access to segments from other segments so that software and data can be protected from interfering with each other.

In compatibility and legacy modes, up to 16,383 unique segments can be defined. The base-address value, segment size (called a limit), protection, and other attributes for each segment are contained in a data structure called a segment descriptor. Collections of segment descriptors are held in descriptor tables. Specific segment descriptors are referenced or selected from the descriptor table using a segment selector register. Six segment-selector registers are available, providing access to as many as six segments at a time.

Figure 3.9 [50] shows an example of segmented memory.

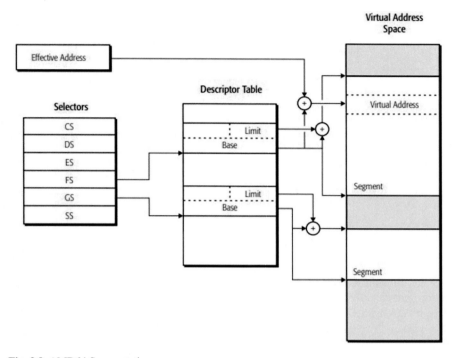

Fig. 3.9 AMD64 Segmentation

One special case of segmented memory is the flat-memory model [50]. In the legacy flat-memory model, all segment-base addresses have a value of 0, and the segment limits are fixed at 4 Gbytes. Segmentation cannot be disabled but use of the flat-memory model effectively disables segment translation. The result is a virtual address that equals the effective address. Figure 3.10[50] shows an example of the flat-memory model.

Software running in 64-bit mode automatically uses the flat-memory model. In 64-bit mode, the segment base is treated as if it were 0, and the segment limit is ignored. This allows an effective addresses to access the full virtual-address space supported by the processor.

3.9.2.2 AMD64 Paging

Paging allows software and data to be relocated in physical-address space using fixed-size blocks called physical pages. The legacy x86 architecture supports three

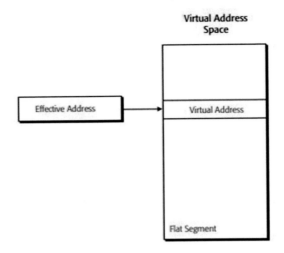

Fig. 3.10 AMD64 Flat Segmentation

different physical-page sizes of 4 Kbytes, 2 Mbytes, and 4 Mbytes [50]. As with
segment translation, access to physical pages by lesserprivileged software can be
restricted.

Page translation uses a hierarchical data structure called a page-translation table
to translate virtual pages into physical-pages. The number of levels in the translation-
table hierarchy can be as few as one or as many as four, depending on the physical-
page size and processor operating mode. Translation tables are aligned on 4-Kbyte
boundaries. Physical pages must be aligned on 4-Kbyte, 2-Mbyte, or 4- Mbyte
boundaries, depending on the physical-page size.

Each table in the translation hierarchy is indexed by a portion of the virtual-
address bits. The entry referenced by the table index contains a pointer to the base
address of the next-lower-level table in the translation hierarchy. In the case of the
lowest-level table, its entry points to the physical-page base address. The physical
page is then indexed by the least-significant bits of the virtual address to yield the
physical address.

Figure 3.11 shows an example of paged memory with three levels in the
translation-table hierarchy

Software running in long mode is required to have page translation enabled.

3.9.2.3 AMD64 Mixing Segmentation and Paging

Memory-management software can combine the use of segmented memory and
paged memory [50]. Because segmentation cannot be disabled, paged-memory management requires some minimum initialization of the segmentation resources. Paging

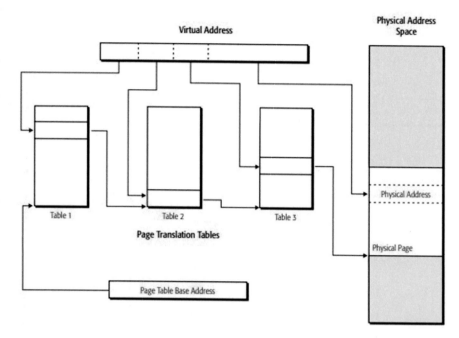

Fig. 3.11 AMD64 Paging

can be completely disabled, so segmentedmemory management does not require initialization of the paging resources.

Segments can range in size from a single byte to 4 Gbytes in length. It is therefore possible to map multiple segments to a single physical page and to map multiple physical pages to a single segment. Alignment between segment and physical-page boundaries is not required, but memory-management software is simplified when segment and physical-page boundaries are aligned.

The simplest, most efficient method of memory management is the flat-memory model. In the flatmemory model, all segment base addresses have a value of 0 and the segment limits are fixed at 4 Gbytes. The segmentation mechanism is still used each time a memory reference is made, but because virtual addresses are identical to effective addresses in this model, the segmentation mechanism is effectively ignored. Translation of virtual (or effective) addresses to physical addresses takes place using the paging mechanism only.

Because 64-bit mode disables segmentation, it uses a flat, paged-memory model for memory management. The 4 Gbyte segment limit is ignored in 64-bit mode. Figure 3.12 shows an example of this model.

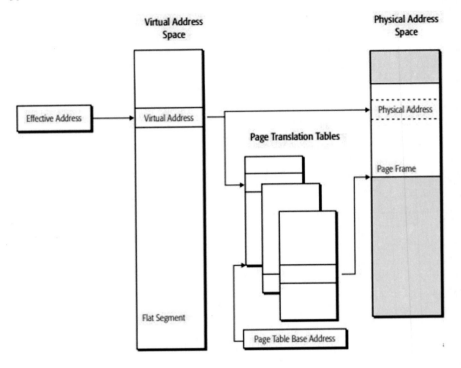

Fig. 3.12 AMD64 Segmentation and Paging

Chapter 4
Databases and the Memory System

Databases today are essential to every business. Whenever you visit a major Web site, such as Google, Ebay, Amazon.com, or thousands of other sites that provide information, there is a database serving up the information requested. Corporations maintain all their important records in databases. Also, Databases are found at the core of many scientific investigations. They represent the data gathered by astronomers, by investigators of the human genome, and by biochemists exploring properties of proteins, among many other scientific activities.

An In-Memory Database Management System is a database management system that predominantly relies on main memory for data storage, management and manipulation. This eliminates the latency and overhead of hard disk storage and reduces the instruction set that's required to access data. To enable more efficient storage and access, the data may be stored in a compressed format.

Traditional DataBase Management Systems move data from disk to memory in a cache or buffer pool when it is accessed. Moving the data to memory makes re-accessing the data more efficient, but the constant need to move data can cause performance issues. Because data in an In-Memory Database Management Systems already resides in memory and doesn't have to be moved, application and query performance can be significantly improved.

In this chapter, we will discuss Database storage techniques used mainly in Relational In-Memory and File Database Management Systems.

4.1 Database Management System

A database is a collection of information that exists over a long period of time, often many years. The term database refers to a collection of data that is managed by a Data Base Management System (DBMS). The DBMS is expected to:

© The Author(s), under exclusive license to Springer Nature Switzerland AG 2022
P. Mejia Alvarez et al., *Main Memory Management on Relational Database Systems*,
SpringerBriefs in Computer Science, https://doi.org/10.1007/978-3-031-13295-7_4

1. Allow users to create new databases and specify their schemas (logical structure of the data), using a specialized data-definition language.
2. Give users the ability to query the data (a query is database question about the data) and modify the data, using an appropriate language, often called a query language or data-manipulation language.
3. Support the storage of very large amounts of data (many terabytes or more) over a long period of time, allowing efficient access to the data for queries and database modifications.
4. Enable durability, the recovery of the database in the face of failures, errors of many kinds, or intentional misuse.
5. Control access to data from many users at once, without allowing unexpected interactions among users (called isolation) and without actions on the data to be performed partially but not completely (called atomicity).

In Figure 4.1 we see an outline of a complete DBMS[16].

At the top of the Figure, there are two distinct sources of commands to the DBMS:

1. Conventional users and application programs that ask for data or modify data.
2. A database administrator: a person or persons responsible for the structure or schema of the database.

4.1.1 Data-Definition Language Commands

The second kind of command is the simpler to process, and we show its trail beginning at the upper right side of Figure 4.1. For example, the database administrator, or DBA, for a university registrar's database[16] might decide that there should be a table or relation with columns for a student, a course the student has taken, and a grade for that student in that course. The DBA might also decide that the only allowable grades are A, B, C, D, and F.

This structure and constraint information is all part of the schema of the database. It is shown in Figure 4.1 as entered by the DBA, who needs special authority to execute schema-altering commands, since these can have profound effects on the database. These schema-altering data-definition language (DDL) commands are parsed by a DDL processor and passed to the execution engine, which then goes through the index/file/record manager to alter the metadata, that is, the schema information for the database.

4.1.2 Query Processing

The great majority of interactions with the DBMS follow the path on the left side of Figure 4.1. A user or an application program initiates some action, using the

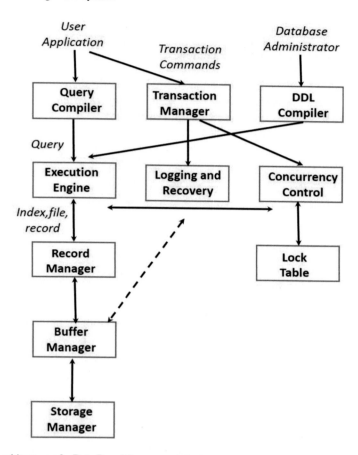

Fig. 4.1 Architecture of a Data Base Management System

data-manipulation language (DML). This command does not affect the schema of the database, but it may affect the content of the database (if the action is a query).

DML statements are handled by two separate subsystems, as follows.

- **Answering the Query**: The query is parsed and optimized by a query compiler. The resulting query plan, or sequence of actions the DBMS will perform to answer the query, is passed to the execution engine. The execution engine issues a sequence of requests for small pieces of data, typically records or tuples of a relation, to a resource manager that knows about data files (holding relations), the format and size of records in those files, and index files, which help find elements of data files quickly.

  The requests for data are passed to the buffer manager. The buffer manager's task is to bring appropriate portions of the data from secondary storage (disk) where it is kept permanently, to the main-memory buffers. Normally, the page or disk block is the unit of transfer between buffers and disk. The buffer manager communicates with a storage manager to get data from disk. The storage manager might involve operating-system commands, but more typically, the DBMS issues commands directly to the disk controller.

- **Transaction Processing**: Queries and other DML actions are grouped into transactions, which are units that must be executed atomically and in isolation from one another. Any query or modification action can be a transaction by itself. In addition, the execution of transactions must be durable, meaning that the effect of any completed transaction must be preserved even if the system fails in some way right after completion of the transaction. We divide the transaction processor into two major parts:

  1. A concurrency-control manager, or scheduler, responsible for assuring atomicity and isolation of transactions, and
  2. A logging and recovery manager, responsible for the durability of transactions.

4.1.3 Storage and Buffer Management

The data of a database normally resides in secondary storage. In today's computer systems secondary storage generally means magnetic disk. However, to perform any useful operation on data, that data must be in main memory. It is the job of the storage manager to control the placement of data on disk and its movement between disk and main memory.

In a simple database system, the storage manager might be nothing more than the file system of the underlying operating system. However, for efficiency purposes, DBMS's normally control storage on the disk directly, at least under some circumstances. The storage manager keeps track of the location of files on the disk and obtains the block or blocks containing a file on request from the buffer manager.

The buffer manager is responsible for partitioning the available main memory into buffers, which are page-sized regions into which disk blocks can be transferred. Thus, all DBMS components that need information from the disk will interact with the buffers and the buffer manager, either directly or through the execution engine. The kinds of information that various components may need include:

1. **Data**: the contents of the database itself.
2. **Metadata**: the database schema that describes the structure of, and constraints on, the database.
3. **Log Records**: information about recent changes to the database; these support durability of the database.
4. **Statistics**: information gathered and stored by the DBMS about data properties such as the sizes of, and values in, various relations or other components of the database.
5. **Indexes**: data structures that support efficient access to the data.

4.1.4 Transaction Processing

It is normal to group one or more database operations into a transaction, which is a unit of work that must be executed atomically and in apparent isolation from other transactions. In addition, a DBMS offers the guarantee of durability: that the work of a completed transaction will never be lost. The transaction manager therefore accepts transaction commands from an application, which tell the transaction manager when transactions begin and end, as well as information about the expectations of the application (some may not wish to require atomicity, for example). The transaction processor performs the following tasks:

1. **Logging**: In order to assure durability, every change in the database is logged separately on disk. The log manager follows one of several policies designed to assure that no matter when a system failure or "crash" occurs, a recovery manager will be able to examine the log of changes and restore the database to some consistent state. The log manager initially writes the log in buffers and negotiates with the buffer manager to make sure that buffers are written to disk (where data can survive a crash) at appropriate times.
2. **Concurrency control**: Transactions must appear to execute in isolation. But in most systems, there will in truth be many transactions executing that the individual actions of multiple transactions are executed in such an order that the net effect is the same as if the transactions had in fact executed in their entirety, one-at-a-time. A typical scheduler does its work by maintaining locks on certain pieces of the database. These locks prevent two transactions from accessing the same piece of data in ways that interact badly. Locks are generally stored in a main-memory lock table, as suggested by Figure 4.1. The scheduler affects the execution of queries and other database operations by forbidding the execution engine from accessing locked parts of the database.
3. **Deadlock resolution**: As transactions compete for resources through the locks that the scheduler grants, they can get into a situation where none can proceed because each needs something another transaction has. The transaction manager has the responsibility to intervene and cancel (rollback or abort) one or more transactions to let the others proceed.

4.1.5 The Query Processor

The portion of the DBMS that most affects the performance that the user sees is the query processor. In Figure 4.1 the query processor is represented by two components:

1. **The query compiler**, which translates the query into an internal form called a query plan. The latter is a sequence of operations to be performed on the data. Often the operations in a query plan are implementations of relational algebra operations. The query compiler consists of three major units:

- **A query parser**, which builds a tree structure from the textual form of the query.
- **A query preprocessor**, which performs semantic checks on the query (e.g., making sure all relations mentioned by the query actually exist), and performing some tree transformations to turn the parse tree into a tree of algebraic operators representing the initial query plan.
- **A query optimizer**, which transforms the initial query plan into the best available sequence of operations on the actual data.

  The query compiler uses metadata and statistics about the data to decide which sequence of operations is likely to be the fastest. For example, the existence of an index, which is a specialized data structure that facilitates access to data, given values for one or more components of that data, can make one plan much faster than another.

2. **The execution engine**, which has the responsibility for executing each of the steps in the chosen query plan. The execution engine interacts with most of the other components of the DBMS, either directly or through the buffers. It must get the data from the database into buffers in order to manipulate that data. It needs to interact with the scheduler to avoid accessing data that is locked, and with the log manager to make sure that all database changes are properly logged.

4.2 In-Memory Data Bases

In main memory database system (MMDB) data resides permanently in main physical memory; while in a conventional database system (DRDB) it is disk resident [64]. In a DRDB, disk data may be cached into memory for access; in a MMDB the memory resident data may have a backup copy on disk. So in both cases, a given object can have copies both in memory and on disk. The key difference is that in MMDB the primary copy lives permanently in memory, and this has important implications (to be discussed) as to how it is structured and accessed.

As semiconductor memory becomes cheaper and chip densities increase, it becomes feasible to store larger and larger databases in memory, making MMDB's a reality. Because data can be accessed directly in memory, MMDB's can provide much better response times and transaction throughputs, as compared to DRDB's. This is especially important for realtime applications where transactions have to be completed by their specified deadlines.

A computer's main memory clearly has different properties from that of magnetic disks, and these differences have profound implications on the design and performance of the database system. Although these differences are well known, it is worthwhile reviewing them briefly[64].

1. The access time for main memory is orders of magnitude less than for disk storage.
2. Main memory is normally volatile, while disk storage is not. However, it is possible (at some cost) to construct nonvolatile main memory.

3. Disks have a high, fixed cost per access that does not depend on the amount of data that is retrieved during the access. For this reason, disks are block-oriented storage devices. Main memory is not block oriented.
4. The layout of data on a disk is much more critical than the layout of data in main memory, since sequential access to a disk is faster than random access. Sequential access is not as important in main memories.
5. Main memory is normally directly accessible by the processor(s), while disks are not. This may make data in main memory more vulnerable than disk resident data to software errors.

These differences have effects on almost every aspect of database management, from concurrency control to application interfaces [64].

4.3 Types of Databases

Over the past fifty years, data management using computerized systems has taken many approaches like:

- Instant small systems that use a single file to store all data.
- File processing systems, that store data in multiple files.
- Relational databases.
- Object databases.
- NoSQL Databases.

Since the seventies (1970), relational database systems have dominated the database system field. However, more recently, object and NoSQL databases have been used to complement the missing gaps of the rational systems [12].

In this chapter, we will discuss only relational databases.

4.3.1 The Object Model

In the object model, a database system uses the object-oriented paradigm to represent information in the form of objects. This approach differs from the relational model which is table-oriented. Object-oriented database management systems try to combine database systems with object-oriented programming languages. Because of this, programmers can maintain consistency within one environment. The OO approach to database design and implementation is preferable for complex applications where relations between the objects is low, as in [12]:

- Computer Aid Design
- Geographic information systems
- Artificial intelligence and expert systems

4.3.2 In-Memory NoSQL Databases

NoSQL is short for Not Only SQL, and a NoSQL database provides a different mechanism from a relational database for data storage and retrieval. Data in NoSQL databases is usually structured as a tree, graph or key-value rather than a tabular relation, and the query language is usually not SQL as well. NoSQL database is motivated by its simplicity, horizontal scaling and finer control over availability, and it usually compromises consistency in favor of availability and partition tolerance [51].

With the trend of "Memory is the new disk", in-memory NoSQL databases are flourishing in recent years. There are key-value stores such as Redis [52], RAMCloud [53], MemepiC [54], Masstree [55], and MICA [64]. Also there are document stores such as MongoDB [56], Couchbase[57], graph databases such as Trinity [58], Bitsy [59], RDF databases such as OWLIM [60] and WhiteDB [61].

There are some systems that are partially in-memory, such as MongoDB [56], MonetDB [62], MDB [63], as they use memory-mapped files to store data such that the data can be accessed as if it was in the memory.

4.4 The Relational Model

On the relational model, a database system is a collection of time-varying relations with desirable constraints and features that enhance the effective and efficient management of the database. The following are some characteristics of relations:

- The relations are conceptualized and implemented as files. Each relation contains one record type. Each relation has a primary key, chosen from a set of candidate keys.
- Each relation type is made up of atomic attributes. Therefore each attribute is defined in a domain (or data type) and can only have valid values within that domain.
- Relations organize in sets containing the same type of relations.

The relational model bases heavily on set theory, and it defines the possible operations that can be exercised with the sets, for example [12]:

- Projection
- Join
- Product
- Union
- Intersect
- Difference

Relational databases implement the operations defined in the relational model.

4.4.1 Relational Database Storage Structures

4.4.1.1 Tables

In a relational database system, tables are used to physically instantiate relations sets. Therefore tables are an unsorted collection of records (or relations) of the same type [13]. The system offers management features for tables, such as:

- Table creation
- Table deletion
- Tuple insertion
- Tuple deletion
- Tuple selection

4.4.1.2 Indexes

Indexes are structures that derive from database tables. They are the answer to the need to optimize access to table records. Tables contain unsorted records. However, indexes organize table's records according to the applications access needs. There are two index families [13]:

- Range indexes, suited to optimize range selection of records.
- Matching indexes, suited to optimize the matching selection of records.

Indexes are a better option than storing the records in a sorted table since they have better performance characteristics on Insertion, deletion, and traversal.

4.4.2 User Interface

The database management system defines a data sub-language (DSL) to operate on data, for example, SQL or Structured Query Language is the industry standard to define tables and access data. DSL is the typical method used as an external user interface; it is concerned specifically with database objects and operations. This characteristic makes it a fourth generation language (4GL) [14].

Data sub-language can be subdivided into the following categories [12]:

- **DDL** or data definition language is used to define all database objects that make up the conceptual schema, e.g., create table statement.
- **DML** or data manipulation language is used to facilitate manipulation of data. DML usually includes a query language, e.g., insert into table statement.
- **DCL** or data control language is used to set up control environments for data management by the end user, e.g., set variable statement.

4.4.3 Database Workload

The workload in a database system is defined as a complete set of requests that the database system receives at a time frame. It does not matter if the petitions are evaluated or executed. The type of petitions that are received by the database system is utterly dependent on the application that lives on top of the database. The workload can be characterized, however, to optimize the access patterns of the database and provide the best performance characteristics to the application. The characterization of database workloads is also used by database administrators to compare all the different database management systems that are commercially available because its quantitative description is a fundamental part of all performance evaluation studies [15]. Some usual types of database workloads are the following:

- **OLTP: Online transaction processing**. Shopping cart applications mainly use OLTP workload.
- **Analytic**: These are read-only systems that store historical data of a business to get reports.
- **Data-driven decision support**: These are systems that integrate inferencing capabilities provided by the management system or use the aggregation function in the database.
- **Batch/ELF**: ELF stands for Efficient, lightweight, fast transactions. This type of applications applies small transactions to a typically huge set of data.

4.5 Database Storage Management

The data stored in a database management system (DBMS) must persist across program executions, machine reboots and database reloads. Therefore it must be stored in external storage devices. However, for the DMBS to be able to operate on the data, it must be in memory.

The basic abstraction of data in a DBMS is a collection of records, or a file, and each file consists of one or more pages. The files and access methods organize data carefully to support fast access to desired subsets of records. Understanding how records are organized is essential to using a database system effectively,

A page is the minimum unit of information on the disk, and all transfers of data between main memory and the secondary storage device have to be are done in one-page units. Typically, the cost of page IO dominates the total cost of all database operations. Therefore, database systems are carefully optimized to minimize this cost [13].

A technique called indexing can help when we have to access a collection of records in multiple ways, in addition to efficiently supporting various kinds of selection. In this section, we introduce indexing, an important aspect of file organization in a DBMS.

4.5.1 Data on External Storage

A DBMS stores vast quantities of data, and the data must persist across program executions. Therefore, data is stored on external storage devices such as disks and tapes, and fetched into main memory as needed for processing. The unit of information read from or written to disk is a page. The size of a page is a DBMS parameter, and typical values are 4KB or 8KB.

The cost of page I/O (input from disk to main memory and output from memory to disk) dominates the cost of typical database operations, and database systems are carefully optimized to rninimize this cost. While the details of how files of records are physically stored on disk and how main memory is utilized are covered bellow in this chapter.

The following statements have guided database development:

- Disks are the most important storage devices.
- Tapes are sequential access devices and force the system to read one page after another.
- Each record in a file has a unique identifier called a record id.
- Data is only read into memory for processing and written to disk for persistence[1].
- Buffer management fetches the page from disk if it is not already in memory.

Data is read into memory for processing, and written to disk for persistent storage, by a layer of software called the buffer manager. When the files and access methods layer (which we often refer to as just the file layer) needs to process a page, it asks the buffer manager to fetch the page, specifying the page's rid. The buffer manager fetches the page from disk if it is not already in memory.

Space on disk is managed by the disk space manager, according to the DBMS software architecture. When the files and access methods layer needs additional space to hold new records in a file, it asks the disk space manager to allocate an additional disk page for the file. It also informs the disk space manager when it no longer needs one of its disk pages. The disk space manager keeps track of the pages in use by the file layer. If a page is freed by the file layer, the space rnanager tracks this, and reuses the space if the file layer requests a new page later on.

4.5.2 File Organization

The file of records is an important abstraction in a DBMS, and is implemented by the files and access methods layer of the code.

A database system can execute the following five main operations in a file:

- Creation

---

[1] This statement is false for In-Memory databases, where all data resides in memory at all times and secondary storage is only accessed for disaster recovery purposes.

- Destruction
- Insertion
- Deletion
- Scan

Scan operation is a special operation that allows the user to step through all the records in a table, one at a time. This scan operation is critical since it is the basis of more complex relational algebra operations, like projections.

The most straightforward table structure is an unordered file or heap. In this scheme, the heap-based table stores its records in random order across the pages of the heap. The database can create a different data structure on top of a table like an index, which is a data structure that organizes data records on disk to optimize certain kinds of retrieval operations [13]. A single collection of records can have multiple indexes using different search keys to optimize different sets of retrieval operations. An index that includes the primary key is called a primary index, and it is guaranteed to not contain duplicates; other indexes are called secondary indexes.

4.5.3 Indexing

An index is a data structure that organizes data records on disk to optimize certain kinds of retrieval operations. An index allows us to efficiently retrieve all records that satisfy search conditions on the search key fields of the index. We can also create additional indexes on a given collection of data records, each with a different search key, to speed up search operations that are not efficiently supported by the file organization used to store the data records.

The term data entry is used to refer to the records stored in an index file. A data entry with search key value k, denoted as k*, contains enough information to locate (one or more) data records with search key value k. We can efficiently search an index to find the desired data entries, and then use these to obtain data records (if these are distinct from data entries).

There are three main alternatives for what to store as a data entry in an index:

1. A data entry h is an actual data record (with search key value k).
2. A data entry is a (k, rid) pair, where rid is the record id of a data record with search key value k.
3. A data entry is a (k. rid-list) pair, where rid-list is a list of record ids of data records with search key value k.

Note that if the index is used to store actual data records. Alternative (1), each entry b is a data record with search key value k. We can think of such an index as a special file organization. Such an indexed file organization can be used instead of, for exarnple, a sorted file or an unordered file of records.

Alternatives (2) and (3), which contain data entries that point to data records, are independent of the file organization that is used for the indexed file (i.e., the file that contains the data records). Alternative (3) offers better space utilization than Alternative (2), but data entries are variable in length, depending on the number of data records with a given search key value.

If we want to build more than one index on a collection of data records- for example, we want to build indexes on both the age and the sal fields for a collection of employee records - at most one of the indexes should use Alternative (1) because we should avoid storing data records multiple times.

4.5.3.1 Clustered Index Organization

A clustered index is a file organization for the underlying data records. Data records can be of any size; hence replicating them is not desirable. Clustered indexes are less expensive to maintain than a fully sorted file. However, they are still expensive to maintain. Clustering should be used with responsibility and only when various queries benefit from it directly [13].

Clustering can be useful in the following scenarios:

- The information in the index search key is enough to resolve the query.
- Several data entries can have the same key value.

4.5.3.2 Composite Search Key

The search key for an index can contain several fields; those search keys are called composite or concatenated keys. Composite keys are useful in the following scenarios:

- Equality queries where each field in the search key bound to a constant.
- An index matches a selection condition if the index can be used to retrieve only the tuples that satisfy the condition.
- Aggregate queries where the index can resolve them.

Composite search key indexes support a broad range of queries because they match more conditions than single search key indexes. This capability increases the opportunities for index-only evaluations. Unfortunately, a composite index needs maintenance in response to any operation that modifies any field in the search key. Also, composite indexes are likely to be larger [13].

4.6 Index Data Structures

There are two basic ways to organize data entries:

- **Hash-based indexes**: In this scheme, records are organized using a hash to find records that have a given search key value quickly. The index structure internally contains a set of buckets. Each bucket consist of at least one primary page and possibly additional secondary pages. The pages store the records identifiers (ids) from the file. The system applies a hash function to the search key to find the bucket that a record belongs to. Note that the search key can be any sequence of fields and it does not need to identify records uniquely. If it does, then the index is called a unique index [16].

- **Tree based indexes**: Tree indexes arrange data records in a sorted order determined by the search key value, and a hierarchical data structure is maintained to map the searches to the data records. On the tree structure there is a root node as an entry point for the searches. The leaf nodes of the tree contain the data entries or record ids. The non-leaf pages contain node pointers separated by search key values. This structure is best for locating all data entries with a search key value in the desired range [16].

4.7 Storing Data: Disks and Files

4.7.1 The Memory Hierarchy

As seen in previous chapters memory is arranged in a hierarchy: At the top, we have the processors registers, then the main memory, after that the secondary memory which consists of disks and finally tertiary storage devices like tapes.

Slower storage devices such as tapes and disks play a significant role in database systems because the amount of data is typically massive and only such devices can completely contain it. However for a system to operate on any data; the data needs to be present in memory.

4.7.2 Disks

Disks support direct access to any desired location. Database applications use disks widely. On them, everything is stored as blocks since the block is the smallest data unit. A disk controller interfaces a disk drive to a computer. It implements commands to read and write a sector.

The unit for data transfer between disk and memory is a block. Data needs to be transferred from disk to memory and vice versa for the DBMS to operate on it. Unfortunately, if a single byte is needed, the entire block is transferred. The time to read a block stored on a disk varies depending on the physical location of the data itself. These observations imply that the time taken for database operations is affected significantly by the organization of data on disks.

In essence, two records frequently used together should also be kept close together. Exploiting record organization on disk so that the system preferably reads or writes records sequentially is very important for reducing the overall IO time of the database system [13].

4.7.3 Redundant Array of Independent Disks

Disks are potential bottlenecks for performance and storage system reliability since they contain mechanical elements. Disks have a much higher rate of failure than any other electronic parts of a computer system. A disk array is an arrangement of several disks, organized to increase performance or improve the reliability of the resulting storage system.

Disks arrays enable:

- Increased performance through data stripping
- Increased reliability through redundancy

RAID or redundant arrays of independent disks are disk arrays that implement a combination of data stripping and redundancy [13].

4.7.3.1 Data Stripping

Data striping is a technique by which data spread across multiple disks. The system segments data into partitions of equal size distributed over multiple disks. The stripping unit is the size of the partition, and the partitions are usually distributed using a simple round robin algorithm.

The result of data stripping is improved read and write performance since the different disks can be accessed concurrently [18].

4.7.3.2 Redundancy

While having more disks used for data stripping increases storage system performance, it also lowers overall storage system reliability (the mean time to failure) since more disks can fail independently. The system increases the reliability of a disk by storing redundant information. If a disk fails, the redundant information is used to reconstruct the data contained on the failed disk. The redundant information can be either stored on a small number of checked disks or distributed uniformly over all the disks. To save space on the disks, most redundant disk systems store the parity bit as its redundant information. In the parity scheme, an extra check disk can be used to recover from the failure of any disk in the array.

The RAID system partitions the disk arrays into reliability groups. A reliability group is a set of disks and a set of check disks [18].

4.7.3.3 Levels of Redundancy

Each system has its requirements for redundancy and performance. Thus a RAID system can be set up using one of the following five specifications offering various compromises between performance and data redundancy [18]:

- **Level 0: Non-redundant RAID system**. Uses only data stripping to increase the maximum bandwidth available.
- **Level 1: Mirrored**. Instead of having one copy of the data, two different disks store identical copies of the data.
- **Level 0+1: Striping and mirroring**. Sometimes also referred to as RAID level 10, it combines stripping and mirroring.
- **Level 2: Error correcting codes**. The stripping unit is a single bit. The redundancy scheme used is hamming code. Due to the stripping unit, all disks require a read operation every time; therefore level 2 shows good performance for workloads with many large requests.
- **Level 3: Bit interleaved parity**. Single check disk with parity information and single bit as the data-stripping unit. This level has the lowest reliability overhead possible, a single disk.
- **Level 4: Block interleaved parity**. Single check disk with parity information and block as the data-stripping unit.
- **Level 5: Block-interleaved distributed parity**. This level evenly distributes the parity information across disks, and the block is the data-striping unit. This level removes the single disk bottleneck of level four. This level shows the best performance for a RAID system.
- **Level 6: P+Q redundancy**. The motivation of this level is to be able to recover from more than one disk failure. The level 6 special capability is particularly useful for huge disk arrays. RAID level 6 uses red-Solomon codes to recover from disk failures.

4.7.3.4 Selecting a RAID Level

The different RAID configurations are useful in different scenarios. Depending on the system requirements, the system administrator can choose one level over another. The following is a summary of how a system designer can choose one level over another [13]:

- **Level 0**: If data loss is not an issue, it improves system performance.
- **Level 0+1**: Useful for small storage subsystems and provides the best write performance.
- **Level 3**: Is appropriate for workloads consisting mainly of large transfer requests of contiguous blocks.
- **Level 5**: It is appropriate for any workload with small or large requests.
- **Level 6**: It is good when higher levels of reliability are required.

4.7.4 Disk Space Management

The disk space manager of a database system supports the concept of a page as a unit of data and provides commands to allocate or deallocate a page or write a page. It is often used to allocate a sequence of pages as a contiguous sequence of blocks to hold data frequently accessed in sequential order. The disk space manager hides all the details of the underlying hardware and allows the upper layer hardware to think of the data as a collection of pages [13]. However, the disk space manager keeps track of used blocks on the disk as well as which pages are on which blocks. It is likely that sub-sequential allocations and deallocations create external fragmentation; however, the holes in the disk can be added to a free list for future use [13] without any user action required.

Typically, an OS supports the disk as a file of sequential bytes that is then translated into reading or write operations to a block on disk. The disk space manager is responsible for managing the space in these OS files if it is built using the operating system.

4.7.5 Buffer Management

The buffer manager is the software layer responsible for bringing pages from disk into main memory as they are needed. To do so the buffer manager partitions the available memory into a collection of pages. The buffer pool is the name of this collection. In addition to the buffer pool, the buffer manager also stores information about each page, like a dirty byte and a pin count. The dirty bit informs the buffer pool that the page has modifications. The pin count contains the count of how many processes are currently using a page. Initially, the dirty bit is off and the pin count is zero for any page. When the system requests a page, the buffer manager does the following:

1. Checks the buffer pool to see if some frame contains the requested page and, if so, increments the pin count of that frame. If the page is not in the pool, the buffer manager brings it in as follows:
2. Chooses a frame for replacement, using the replacement policy, and increments its pin count.
3. If the dirty bit for the replacement frame is on, writes the page it contains to disk (that is, the disk copy of the page is overwritten with the contents of the frame).
4. Reads the requested page into the replacement frame.
5. Returns the (main memory) address of the frame containing the requested page to the requestor.

Incrementing the pin count is called pinning, and decrementing it is called unpinning. The buffer manager will not read another page into the frame until its pin count is zero [13].

4.7.5.1 Buffer Replacement Policies

In the operating systems world, the best-known replacement policy is least recently used (LRU). However, LRU and its approximations algorithms discussed previously are not always the best replacement strategies for a database system; this is especially true if many users require sequential scans of the same data [16].

Suppose that a scan requires at least one more page than what is available in the buffer pool. In this situation, every scan will read every page from disk. In fact, LRU is the worst possible page replacement strategy for this situation. The problem is called sequential flooding.

Other replacement policies are: first in first out (FIFO) and most recently used (MRU). For the scan operation, MRU is the ideal policy [13].

4.7.5.2 Buffer Management in DBMS vs OS

Many similarities exist between the problems exposed in the virtual memory section and the ones faced by the buffer management system of a database. A DBMS can often predict reference patterns because most page references generate from higher-level operations like scans or other relational algebra operations. The ability to predict the access pattern allows for far better choices of pages for replacement and makes the idea of specialized buffer replacement policies more attractive. Since the buffer manager can anticipate the next several pages requested, prefetching becomes very relevant. If a page is pre-fetched correctly, it will be available in the buffer pool when the system requests it. This behavior is something that was very complicated in virtual memory layer but trivial at the DBMS level.

Another available strategy with the anticipation of the future is to read contiguous blocks of memory into the buffer pool, which is much faster than reading them independently.

A DBMS also requires the ability to explicitly force a page to disk, since it needs warranties that the copy on disk is up to date with the copy in memory. In fact, the WAL protocol requires the ability to order how specific pages in the buffer pool are persisted on disk before other pages for adequately handling crash recovery of the system.

4.7.6 Data Storage Implementation

We will discuss now about the way pages are stored on disk and brought into main memory to the way pages are used to store records and organized into logical collections or files. Higher levels of the DBMS code treat a page as effectively being a collection of records, ignoring the representation and storage details. In fact, the concept of a collection of records is not limited to the contents of a single page; a file can span several pages. In this section, we consider how a collection of pages can be organized as a file. We discuss how the space on a page can be organized to store a collection of records.

4.7.6.1 Heap File Implementation

The data in the pages of a heap file have no particular order, and the only guarantee that one can retrieve all records in the file is by repeating requests for the next record. Every record has a unique record id, and every page in a file is of the same size. Supported operations in a heap file include the following:

- Create the heap.
- Destroy the heap.
- Insert a record.
- Delete a record with a given record id.
- Get a record with a given record id.
- Scan all records in the heap file.

The DBMS needs to keep track of which records are in each heap file to implement scan efficiently. It also needs to keep track of the free space in the heap to implement insert efficiently [13].

Linked List of Pages

A heap can be implemented using a double linked list of pages. An important task that uses it is to maintain information about the empty slots that exist, or the creation and the deleting of records from the heap file.

Here, the following two issues need a solution:

- Keep track of free spaces on a page.
- Keep track of pages with free space.

When a new page is required, the following steps execute:

1. Request a block from the disk space manager.
2. Format the block as a heap page.
3. Add the heap page to the linked list of pages in the heap file.

When the system deletes a page from a heap file, the following steps execute:

- The heap page is removed from the linked list of pages.
- The disk space manager is requested to deallocate the block where the heap page resides.

Directory of Pages

A directory is a collection of pages. The DBMS then only needs to remember where the first directory page of each heap file is. One way to implement the directory is an array of pointers to heap pages, where each directory entry identifies a page or a sequence of pages in the heap file (Figure 4.2). As the heap grows, the number of pages in the directory grows as well. The system can manage free space by maintaining an empty bit per page and a counter indicating the amount of free space on the page.

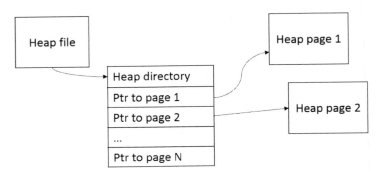

Fig. 4.2 Heap directory

4.7.7 Page Formats

In general, a page is a collection of slots and each slot contains a record. A pair identifies a record:

- Page Id.
- Record number.

The purpose of the record id is to identify a record across the entire database uniquely. The id itself could have more fields according to the database needs to accomplish the required goal.

4.7.8 Fixed Length Records

The records on a page are guaranteed to be of the same length when using this scheme. Thus, records can be placed array-wise, consecutively on the page. At any instant, records are occupied or unoccupied [13]. An empty slot must be found and placed there to insert a record. The main issues are:

- how to keep track of empty records?
- how to locate all records on a page?

There are two common strategies for solving these issues:

- A bitmap of the used records can be kept to track whether a record is in use or available for an insert.
- The first N records should always be kept occupied. Therefore the slots from N to the last slot available on the page are free.

4.7.9 Variable Length Records

The most flexible organization for variable length records is to maintain a directory of slots for each page with the following pair per slot:

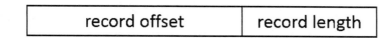

Fig. 4.3 Variable length page metadata

The space available for new records must be managed carefully because page pre-formatting into slots is not universal. One way to solve this issue is to keep a pointer to the start of the free segment of the page [13]. When a record is too big to fit on the page due to fragmentation, the system can reclaim space so that all existing records on the page can fit contiguously. This organization is also used for fixed length records if they need to be moved around frequently.

4.7.10 Record Formats

In this section, we discuss how to organize fields within a record. While choosing a way to organize the fields of a record, we must take into account whether the fields of the record are of fixed or variable length and consider the cost of various operations on the record, including retrieval and modification of fields.

4.7.10.1 Fixed Length Records

In this scheme, the system for each field of the record has a fixed length, and there is a fixed number of fields (Figure 4.4) . The fields of any record are always contiguous, and the address of the fields can be calculated using the length of the fields that come before it [16].

Heap page header				
Field 1	Field 2	Field 3	Field 4	....
Record 2				
...				
Record N				

Fig. 4.4 Heap page containing fixed length records

Fixed length record strategy is similar to the slab allocator studied in section 3.8.8.2.

4.7.10.2 Variable Length Records

A record can be of variable size if one of the fields is of variable size, or the number of fields in the record can vary. The later, however, is not allowed in relational algebra.

One possible file organization is to store the fields consecutively and use a particular symbol as a separator (Figure 4.5). Alternatively, space can be reserved at the beginning of the block to store the offset of the beginning of the fields, so that the i'th integer is the offset to the beginning of the i'th field of the record [16].

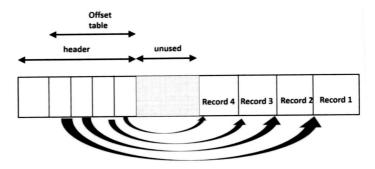

Fig. 4.5 Variable length record format

4.8 Tree Structured Indexes

Tree-based indexes also provide support for equality selections although not as good as a hash-based indexed. This type of indexes excel in range selections. The B+Tree is a dynamic structure that adjusts to changes in the file gracefully. It is the most widely used index structure because it adjusts well to changes.

4.8.1 Indexed Sequential Access Method (ISAM)

The ISAM tree structure stores data entries as follows:

, • The data entries of the ISAM index are in the pre-allocated leaf pages of the tree.
• Additional overflow pages chained to a leaf page can be added if needed.

Databases carefully organize the layout of pages so that they correspond to the physical characteristics of the disk or the underlying storage device. The ISAM structure is static. When the system creates the file, all leaf pages are allocated sequentially and sorted by the search key value.

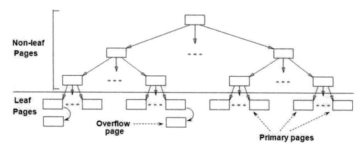

Fig. 4.6 ISAM index structure

The system then allocates the non-leaf pages, and if there are subsequent inserts into the file such that the page space is exhausted, there is an overflow area exists for allocating subsequent pages.

4.8.1.1 Performance Considerations of ISAM Indexes

Once the system creates the ISAM, the subsequent inserts and deletes affect only contents of the leaf pages. Therefore long overflow pages can be created and considerably affect the performance of the operations in the index.

The fact that only leaf pages are modified is an advantage for concurrent access because it grants that the index structure will not be modified while traversing the index. This also means that the structure needs to be locked for shorter periods, only while accessing a leaf node. If the data distribution and size are relatively static so that overflow chains are rare, ISAM tree is a good option [13]. Database systems do not use ISAM indexes anymore in modern architectures because of this limitation.

4.8.2 B+Trees

The B+Tree is a widely used search tree structure. It is a balanced tree in which its internal nodes direct the search, and the leaf nodes contain all the data entries or keys. The following are the main characteristics of the B+Tree:

- The tree structure grows dynamically. It is not possible to allocate pages sequentially.
- Leaf pages are linked using page pointer for efficient scan operation.
- Inserts and deletes keep it balanced.
- The algorithms guarantees a minimum occupancy of 50% for each node except the root, therefore it is a dense structure.
- Searching for a record only requires a traversal from the root to 1 leaf.
- B+Trees are likely to perform better than ISAM trees.

In B+Trees, every node contains m entries, where d <= m <= 2d and the value is called the order of the tree and measures the capacity of a node. The ordering concept of B+Trees usually needs to be relaxed in practice to fit physical space criteria related to the underlying storage devices [16].

The formatting of a node is the same as for ISAM: Non-leaf nodes contain m index entries and contain m+1 pointers to children. Besides, leaf nodes contain data entries [13].

Operations of the B+Trees are the following:

- **Search a key**: Suppose we have a B Tree index and we want to find a record with the search key of the index. To do so, we need to recursively call the search node function into the appropriate child node until the appropriate leaf node is reached. Reference shows the pseudocode for this operation.
- **Insert a Key**: The basic idea is to recursively call the insert function into the appropriate child node until it reaches the appropriate leaf node. For a B+Tree insert, the system needs to find the leaf node where it needs to belong. If the node that needs to hold the entry is full, a split of the node is required. If a node splits, the parent node metadata gets an entry pointing to the new node. A B+Tree node is full when we try to insert the 2d+1 element into the node. The node then splits in half, and the middle key goes to the parent node up the tree. Reference [13] shows the pseudocode for this operation.
- **Delete a Key**: The basic idea is to recursively call the delete function into the appropriate child node until it reaches the appropriate leaf node. For a delete operation from the tree, the system needs to find the leaf node that contains the entry. If the node that contains the entry does not meet the minimum node occupancy, a merge of two nodes is required. If two nodes are merged, its parent needs to be updated. Reference [13] shows the pseudocode for this operation.

4.9 Hash Based Indexes

Hash indexes use a hashing function to map values from the search field to a range of bucket numbers to find the page on which the desired entry belongs. There are various hash indexing schemes like

- Static hashing. It is similar to ISAM tree-based indexing.
- Extendible Hashing. It uses a directory to support insert and delete efficiently with no overflow pages.
- Linear Hashing. It uses a policy for bucket creation that supports inserts and deletes efficiently without using a directory.

Hash indexes do not support range scans. However, they have proved to be very efficient in implementing other relational algebra operations like joins. The index nested loop join method uses many equality selections queries, and the cost difference between the hash index and tree indexes can be significant [13].

4.9.1 Static Hashing

Pages containing data form a collection of buckets. There is only one original page, and possibly multiple additional overflow pages, per bucket.

The system applies a hash function h to search for data entries. The hash function enables the system to identify the bucket where it belongs and then search the bucket. The system could store the data entries sorted to speed up the searches. The hash function is also used to identify the correct bucket to place data in when inserting data entries. If the page is full, an overflow page needs to be allocated and chained to the primary page for inserting the entry. The hash function is also used to identify the correct bucket when deleting data entries. The system searches the bucket for the entry, and if it finds it, the record is finally deleted. If the data entry happened to be the last one on an overflow page, the system also deleted the overflow page. A list of free pages can be kept for future use or reclaim.

Since the system knows the number of buckets when it creates the static hash index, the primary pages can be stored contiguously on disk. Unfortunately, this also restricts the number of buckets.

If a file shrinks considerably, the space in the file is wasted, and if the file grows, the overflow pages can grow unbounded, resulting in performance deterioration [13].

4.9.2 Extensible Hashing

Extensible hashing tries to solve the need to add overflow pages from static hashing. To do so, it needs to reorganize the file by doubling the number of buckets. A directory of pointers to buckets is used to double the size of the file without needing to read every bucket and write the double of each one. Finally, it only needs to split the bucket that overflowed. Using this technique to double the file calls for allocating a new bucket page and writing the new and old buckets. The directory is much smaller than the complete file itself since each element on it is a page id and can be doubled only by copying it over.

The basic technique used by extensible hashing is to treat the result of applying a hash function as a number and interpret the last d bits (where d depends on the size of a directory) as an offset from the directory, and it needs to be stored and incremented every time the directory doubles.

In summary, data entries can be found by computing their hash value, then taking the last d bits to look at the buckets pointed to by this directory element.

For deletes, the system locates and deletes the data entries. If a bucket is empty, it can be merged. However, this step is often omitted [13].

4.9.3 Linear Hashing

Linear hashing is another dynamic hashing technique; however, it does not require a directory. It uses a family of hash functions h1, h2, h3... with the property that each function range is twice the one of its predecessor [13].

Chapter 5
Database Systems: Real Examples

Relational databases have been developed and enhanced since 1970s, and the relational model has been dominating in almost all large-scale data processing applications since early 1990s. Some widely used relational databases include Oracle, IBM DB2, MySQL and PostgreSQL. In relational databases, data is organized into tables/relations, and ACID properties are guaranteed. More recently, a new type of relational databases, called NewSQL (e.g., Google Spanner [8], H-Store [29]) has emerged. These systems seek to provide the same scalability as NoSQL databases for OLTP while still maintaining the ACID guarantees of traditional relational database systems.

Other examples of commercial in-memory relational databases include SAP HANA [23], VoltDB [24], Oracle TimesTen [25], SolidDB [26], IBM DB2 with BLU Acceleration [27], Microsoft Hekaton [28], NuoDB [30], eXtremeDB [31], Pivotal SQLFire [32], and MemSQL [33]. There are also well known research/open-source projects such as HStore [34], HyPer [35], Silo [36], Crescando [37], HYRISE [38], and MySQL Cluster NDB [39].

In this chapter we focus in TimesTen [25], MySQL [19], H-Store / VoltDB [24], Hekaton [28], HyPer/ScyPer [35], and SAP Hana [23] Data Base Systems.

5.1 TimesTen In-Memory Database

Oracle TimesTen In-Memory Database is a memory optimized relational database that provides applications with extremely fast response time and very high throughput. Oracle TimesTen In-Memory Database (TimesTen) delivers real-time performance by changing the assumptions around where data resides at run time. By managing data in memory, and optimizing data structures and access algorithms accordingly, database operations execute with maximum efficiency. TimesTen deployments

© The Author(s), under exclusive license to Springer Nature Switzerland AG 2022
P. Mejia Alvarez et al., *Main Memory Management on Relational Database Systems*,
SpringerBriefs in Computer Science, https://doi.org/10.1007/978-3-031-13295-7_5

commonly have multi-user and multi-threaded applications using row-level locking and read-committed isolation. Applications access TimesTen databases using standard SQL via JDBC, ODBC, ODP.NET, OCI (Oracle Call Interface), Pro*C/C++, and Oracle PL/SQL programming interfaces. Running TimesTen linked with the application achieves the best performance (also known as "direct mode"). However conventional client/server access is commonly used when several applications running on different servers share a database. TimesTen databases are persistent and recoverable. A combination of transaction logging and database checkpointing to disk enables durability. High Availability is provided using TimesTen Replication to replicate transactions between TimesTen databases in real-time. Most enterprise deployments add TimesTen Replication for availability and disaster recovery. For example, telecommunications and web-accessible global systems such as online-charging, subscriber session management, e-commerce, online stores, travel and reservation websites cannot tolerate application/service downtime; financial services and securities trading systems must remain continuously available while financial markets are open. TimesTen Replication uses memory-optimized, transaction log-based replication technology over a network efficient and stream-based protocol for high performance, reliability, and robustness.

Key features of TimesTen include:

- Asynchronous replication, providing maximum performance, and completely decoupling the application from the subscriber receipt process of replicated elements.
- Synchronous replication, providing a higher level of confidence for data consistency between the active and standby databases; the application blocks until the replicated transaction has been both received and committed on the standby database.
- Hot read availability in the standby database; additional read capacity can be provided by configuring additional read-only subscribers.
- Parallel replication for applications that require very high transaction throughput.
- Automated failure detection and failover to the standby database.
- Online upgrades, allowing individual servers to be taken offline for software upgrades, while other servers continue uninterrupted.

5.1.1 Overview

TimesTen has many familiar database features as well as some unique features. The following is a non-comprehensive list of them:

- **TimesTen API support**: The run time architecture of TimesTen supports connectivity through the ODBC, JDBC, OCI, Pro*C/C++ Precompiler and ODP.NET APIs. TimesTen also provides built-in procedures, utilities and the TTClasses API (C++) that extend ODBC, JDBC and OCI functionality for TimesTen-specific operations, as well as supporting SQL and PL/SQL.

- **Access Control**: Allow only users with specific privileges to access particular TimesTen database features.
- **Database connectivity**: TimesTen supports direct driver connections for higher performance, as well as connections through a driver manager. TimesTen also supports client/server connections.
- **Durability**: TimesTen achieves durability through a combination of transaction logging and periodic refreshes of a disk-resident version of the database. Log records are written to disk asynchronously or synchronously to the completion of the transaction and controlled by the application at the transaction level.
- **Performance through query optimization**: TimesTen has a cost-based query optimizer that chooses the best query execution plan based on factors such as the:
  Presence of indexes.
  Cardinality of tables.
  ORDER BY query instructions.
- **Concurrency**: TimesTen provides full support for shared databases. Options are available so users can choose the optimum balance between response time, throughput and transaction semantics for an application.
  Read-committed isolation provides nonblocking operations and is the default isolation level.
  For databases with rigorous transaction semantics, serializable isolation is available.
- **Database character sets and globalization support**: TimesTen provide globalization support for storing, retrieving, and processing data in native languages.
- **In-memory columnar compression**: TimesTen provides the ability to compress tables at the column level, thus storing the data more efficiently. This mechanism provides space reduction for tables by eliminating the redundant storage of duplicate values within columns and improves the performance of SQL queries that perform full table scans.
- **Data replication between servers**: TimesTen replication enables real-time data replication between servers for high availability and load sharing.
- **Business intelligence and online analytical processing**: TimesTen provides analytic SQL functions and aggregate SQL functions for business intelligence and similar applications.
- **Large objects**: Data aging is an operation to remove data that is no longer needed. There are two general types of data aging: removing old data based on some time value or removing data that has been least recently used (LRU).
- **Automatic data aging**: Data aging is an operation to remove data that is no longer needed. There are two general types of data aging: removing old data based on some time value or removing data that has been least recently used (LRU).
- **System monitoring, administration, and utilities**.

5.1.2 Memory Management

TimesTen is a memory resident database; therefore, the complete database must fit in the computer system memory. TimesTen reserves a shared memory segment that is used to store the following database areas:

- **Database metadata**: It contains general information about the database, as well as required information for the database connections and bookkeeping.
- **Database transaction log**: The system keeps an in-memory transaction log for increased performance. It is flushed to disk and used for crash recovery and replication.
- **Database permanent segment**: The permanent database segment is the memory area reserved to store the system and user's objects, e.g., tables, indexes and other parts of the database schema.
- **Temporary database segment**: The temporary database segment is the memory area reserved to work on the database operations during query execution. All the data inside the temporary segment does not survive after system failures and crash recovery.

5.1.2.1 Memory Blocks

The very first memory organization for the permanent and temporary segments in the TimesTen database is using linked lists of blocks. The memory blocks can vary in size, from a minimum lower limit; however, the blocks should be multiples of the underlying disk block size. All database objects map into blocks.

5.1.2.2 TimesTen Heap

To implement tables and indexes, TimesTen uses unsorted heap files organized by a dictionary, as explained on 4.4.2. The unsorted heaps contained heap buffers, which can be of variable length and are organized using a directory. The technique used for the directory is described in chapter 4.7.6.1 The TimesTen heaps and the TimesTen heap buffers are allocated from memory blocks, to preserve memory organization and to be able to store them on disk easily.

5.1.2.3 Records Format

TimesTen records are organized into record pages. Each record page has the following characteristics:

- It contains 256 records for row major organization.
- It is allocated from a heap buffer.
- It can be either temporary or permanent

- It is logged into the transaction log.

All TimesTen records are variable in length, using the technique described in chapter 4.7.10.1.

5.2 MySQL Database

MySQL, the most popular Open Source SQL database management system, is developed, distributed, and supported by Oracle Corporation.

The MySQL database delivers a fast, multi-threaded, multi-user, and robust SQL (Structured Query Language) database server. MySQL Server is intended for mission-critical, heavy-load production systems as well as for embedding into any mass-deployed software. The MySQL software is Dual Licensed. Users can choose to use the MySQL software as an Open Source product under the terms of the GNU General Public License or can purchase a standard commercial license from Oracle [19].

5.2.1 Background

The MySQL database was created in 1979 by a company called TcX as a low-level storage engine with reporting capabilities. It was originally called Unireg.

During the 90's decade, some of TcX customers were asking for SQL capabilities out of Unireg, therefore in 1996 MySQL was released. It offered a subset of the SQL language, an optimizer, and support for various API's but it lacked transactional capabilities, foreign keys, and other somewhat advanced functionality. In the year 2000, an independent company called MySQL AB was formed and established a partnership with SleepyCat to provide a SQL interface for BerkeleyDB data files. Since BerkelyDB supported transactions, the partnership would give transaction support to MySQL.

The code integration for the partnership never really worked out since the BerkelyDB tables were not stable at the time. However, it made the MySQL codebase fully equipped with hooks to easily plug-in new storage engines. The original MySQL storage engine was called MyISAM.

During 2001, the InnoDB storage engine integrated into MySQL. It supported transactions and row-level locking. The integration came out as the MySQL version 4.0 release. During the following years, additional features were added to the MySQL database as well as improved the stability of their releases. In fact, that was the reason why MySQL version 5.0 released during 2003. During 2008 MySQL AB was acquired by Sun Microsystems which was then acquired by Oracle corporation during 2010, which, since 2005, was already owner of Innobase Oy, the company developing the InnoDB storage engine for MySQL [20].

5.2.2 Architecture

The following is a non-comprehensive list of the MySQL database modules from the server side:

- **Server Initialization Module**: During server initialization, it parses the configuration file and the command-line arguments, allocates global memory buffers, initializes global variables and structures, loads the access control tables, and performs a number of other initialization tasks.
- **Connection Manager**: When a client connects, it handles low-level network protocol tasks and handles the control to the thread manager.
- **Thread Manager**: It supplies a thread to handle the connection. The connection thread might be created or retrieved from the thread cache and called to active duty.
- **User Authentication**: Verifies the credentials of the connecting user and allows the client to issue requests.
- **Command Dispatcher**: It handles MySQL native commands or redirected to a specialized module.
- **Parser**: It is responsible for parsing queries and generating a parse tree.
- **Query Cache module**: It caches query results, and tries to short-circuit the execution of queries by delivering the cached result whenever possible.
- **Logging module**: It is responsible for maintaining logical logs. A storage engine may additionally maintain its own lower-level (physical or logical) logs for its purposes, but the Logging Module would not be concerned with those. The logical logs at this point include the binary update log (replication logs), command log (used mostly for server monitoring), and slow query log (used for tracking down poorly optimized queries).
- **Optimizer**: It is responsible for creating the best strategy to answer the query, and executing it to deliver the result to the client.
- **Table Manager**: It is responsible for creating, reading, and modifying the table definition files (.frm extension), maintaining a cache of table descriptors called table cache, and managing table-level locks.
- **Table Modification**: It is responsible for operations such as creating, deleting, renaming, dropping, updating, or inserting into a table.
- **Table Maintenance**: It is responsible for table maintenance operations such as check, repair, back up, restore, defragment, and analyze statistics.
- **Status Reporting**: It is responsible for answering queries about server configuration settings, performance tracking variables, table structure information, replication progress, the condition of the table cache, etc.
- **Replication Module**: It is responsible for delivering a continuous feed of replication log events to the slave upon request. The role of the slave is to retrieve updates from the master and apply them.
- **Access Control**: It verifies that the client user has sufficient privileges to perform the requested operation.

- **Abstracted Storage Engine Interface (Table Handler)**: This module is an abstract class named handler and a structure called a handlerton.
- **Storage Engine Implementations** (MyISAM, InnoDB, MEMORY, Berkeley DB): Each storage engine provides a standard interface for its operations by extending the handler class. The methods of the derived class define the standard interface operations concerning the low-level calls of the specific storage engine.
- **Core API**: It provides functionality for portable file I/O, memory management, string manipulation, filesystem navigation, formatted printing, a rich collection of data structures and algorithms.

Figure 5.1 diagram shows the relations between the server side modules of a MySQL database.

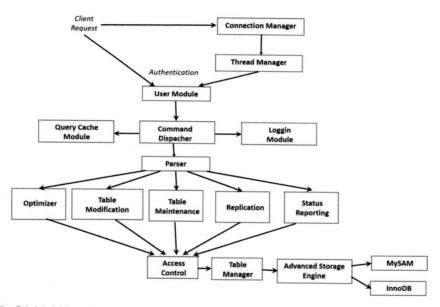

Fig. 5.1 MySQL Architecture

5.2.3 Storage Engines

Different storage engines have different capabilities. The table in figure 5.2 contains a comparison of different storage engines.

For the rest of this section we will be focusing on MySQL using the InnoDB storage engine, since it is the default and most feature rich storage engine in modern MySQL installations.

	MyISAM	InnoDB	Memory	Merge	NDB	Archive	Federated
Transactions	No	Yes	No	No	Yes	No	No
Indexing	B-tree, R-tree, full text	B-tree	Hash, B-tree	B-tree, R-tree	Hash, B-tree	None	Depends on the remote table engine
Storage	Local disk	Local disk	RAM	Local disk	Remote and local cluster nodes	Local disk	Remote MySQLserver instance
Caching	Key cache	Key and data cache	N/A	Same as MyISAM	Key and data cache	None	Depends on the remote table engine
Locking	Table	Row	Table	Table	Row	Row	Relies on the remote table engine
Foreign keys	No	Yes	No	No	No	No	Depends on the remote table engine

Fig. 5.2 Different MySQL storage engines

5.2.3.1 The InnoDB Storage Engine

InnoDB is one of the most complex storage engines currently present in MySQL. It supports transactions, multi-versioning, row-level locks, and foreign keys. It has an extensive system for managing I/O and memory. It has internal mechanisms for deadlock detection and performs a quick and reliable crash recovery. InnoDB uses tablespaces. A tablespace can be stored in a file or on a raw partition. All tables could end up in one common tablespace, or every table may have its own tablespace. The engine stores the data in a particular structure called a clustered index, which is a B+Tree with the primary key acting as the search key value and the actual record. The disk stores the B+Tree. However, when buffering an index page, InnoDB will build an adaptive hash index in memory to speed up the index lookups for the cached page. InnoDB buffers both b-tree keys and data. To locate keys in a page efficiently, InnoDB maintains an additional structure known as the page directory. It is a sparse sorted array of pointers to keys within the page. The system uses a binary search to locate a given record. Afterward, since the index is sparse, it may still be necessary to examine a few more keys in the linked list of records.

5.3 H-Store / VoltDB Data Base Systems

H-Store [34] or its commercial version VoltDB [24] is a distributed row-based in-memory relational database targeted for high-performance OLTP processing. It is motivated by two observations: first, certain operations in traditional disk-based databases, such as logging, latching, locking, B-tree and buffer management operations, incur substantial amount of the processing time (more than 90 percent) when ported to in-memory databases; second, it is possible to re-design in-memory database processing so that these components become unnecessary. In H-Store, most of these "heavy" components are removed or optimized, in order to achieve high-performance transaction processing.

Transaction execution in H-Store is based on the assumption that all (at least most of) the templates of transactions are known in advance, which are represented as a set of compiled stored procedures inside the database. This reduces the overhead of transaction parsing at runtime, and also enables pre-optimizations on the database design and light-weight logging strategy. In particular, the database can be more easily partitioned to avoid multi-partition transactions, and each partition is maintained by a site, which is single-threaded daemon that processes transactions serially and independently without the need for heavy-weight concurrency control (e.g., lock) in most cases. Next, we will elaborate on its transaction processing, data overflow and fault-tolerance strategies.

5.3.1 Transaction Processing

Transaction processing in H-Store is conducted on the partition/site basis [34]. A site is an independent transaction processing unit that executes transactions sequentially, which makes it feasible only if a majority of the transactions are single-sited. This is because if a transaction involves multiple partitions, all these sites are sequentialized to process this distributed transaction in collaboration (usually 2PC), and thus cannot process transactions independently in parallel. H-Store designs a skewaware partitioning model — Horticulture — to automatically partition the database based on the database schema, stored procedures and a sample transaction workload, in order to minimize the number of multi-partition transactions and meanwhile mitigate the effects of temporal skew in the workload. Horticulture employs the large-neighborhood search (LNS) approach to explore potential partitions in a guided manner, in which it also considers read-only table replication to reduce the transmission cost of frequent remote access, secondary index replication to avoid broadcasting, and stored procedure routing attributes to allow an efficient routing mechanism for requests.

The Horticulture partitioning model can reduce the number of multi-partition transactions substantially, but not entirely. The concurrency control scheme must therefore be able to differentiate single partition transactions from multi-partition transactions, such that it does not incur high overhead where it is not needed (i.e., when there are only single-partition transactions). H-Store designs two low overhead concurrency control schemes, i.e., light-weight locking and speculative concurrency control. Light-weight locking scheme reduces the overhead of acquiring locks and detecting deadlock by allowing single-partition transactions to execute without locks when there are no active multi-partition transactions. And speculative concurrency control scheme can proceed to execute queued transactions speculatively while waiting for 2PC to finish (precisely after the last fragment of a multi-partition transaction has been executed), which outperforms the locking scheme as long as there are few aborts or few multi-partition transactions that involve multiple rounds of communication.

In addition, based on the partitioning and concurrency control strategies, H-Store utilizes a set of optimizations on transaction processing, especially for workload with interleaving of single- and multi-transactions. In particular, to process an incoming transaction (a stored procedure with concrete parameter values), H-Store uses a Markov model- based approach to determine the necessary optimizations by predicting the most possible execution path and the set of partitions that it may access. Based on these predictions, it applies four major optimizations accordingly, namely (1) execute the transaction at the node with the partition that it will access the most; (2) lock only the partitions that the transaction accesses; (3) disable undo logging for non-aborting transactions; (4) speculatively commit the transaction at partitions that it no longer needs to access.

5.3.2 Data Overflow

While H-Store is an in-memory database, it also utilizes a technique, called anti-caching, to allow data bigger than the memory size to be stored in the database, without much sacrifice of performance, by moving cold data to disk in a transactionally-safe manner, on the tuple-level, in contrast to the page-level for OS virtual memory management. In particular, to evict cold data to disk, it pops the least recently used tuples from the database to a set of block buffers that will be written out to disks, updates the evicted table that keeps track of the evicted tuples and all the indexes, via a special eviction transaction. Besides, nonblocking fetching is achieved by simply aborting the transaction that accesses evicted data and then restarting it at a later point once the data is retrieved from disks, which is further optimized by executing a pre-pass phase before aborting to determine all the evicted data that the transaction needs so that it can be retrieved in one go without multiple aborts.

5.3.3 Fault Tolerance

H-Store uses a hybrid of fault-tolerance strategies, i.e., it utilizes a replica set to achieve high availability [34], and both checkpointing and logging for recovery in case that all the replicas are lost. In particular, every partition is replicated to k sites, to guarantee k-safety, i.e., it still provides availability in case of simultaneous failure of k sites. In addition, H-Store periodically checkpoints all the committed database states to disks via a distributed transaction that puts all the sites into a copy-onwrite mode, where updates/deletes cause the rows to be copied to a shadow table. Between the interval of two checkpointings, command logging scheme is used to guarantee the durability by logging the commands (i.e., transaction/stored procedure identifier and parameter values), in contrast to logging each operation (insert/delete/ update) performed by the transaction as the traditional ARIES physiological logging does. Besides, memory-resident undo log can be used to support rollback for some abort-able transactions. It is obvious that command logging has a much lower runtime overhead than physiological logging as it does less work at runtime and writes less data to disk, however, at the cost of an increased recovery time. Therefore, command logging scheme is more suitable for short transactions where node failures are not frequent.

5.4 Hekaton Data Base System

Hekaton [28] is a memory-optimized OLTP engine fully integrated into Microsoft SQL server, where Hekaton tables [1] and regular SQL server tables can be accessed at the same time, thereby providing much flexibility to users. It is designed for high-concurrency OLTP, with utilization of lock-free or latch-free data structures (e.g., latch-free hash and range indexes), and an optimistic MVCC technique. It also incorporates a framework, called Siberia, to manage hot and cold data differently, equipping it with the capacity to handle Big Data both economically and efficiently.

Furthermore, to relieve the overhead caused by interpreter-based query processing mechanism in traditional databases, Hekaton adopts the compile-once-and-execute-many-times strategy, by compiling SQL statements and stored procedures into C code first, which will then be converted into native machine code [28]. Specifically, an entire query plan is collapsed into a single function using labels and gotos for code sharing, thus avoiding the costly argument passing between functions and expensive function calls, with the fewest number of instructions in the final compiled binary. In addition, durability is ensured in Hekaton by using incremental checkpoints, and transaction logs with log merging and group commit optimizations, and availability is achieved by maintaining highly available replicas [28].

We shall next elaborate on its concurrency control, indexing and hot/cold data management.

5.4.1 Multi-version Concurrency Control

Hekaton adopts optimistic MVCC to provide transaction isolation without locking and blocking. Basically, a transaction is divided into two phases, i.e., normal processing phase where the transaction never blocks to avoid expensive context switching, and validation phase where the visibility of the read set and phantoms are checked [2], and then outstanding commit dependencies are resolved and logging is enforced. Specifically, updates will create a new version of record rather than updating the ex-

---

[1] Hekaton tables are declared as "memory optimized" in SQL server, to distinguish with normal tables.

[2] Some of validation checks are not necessary, depending on the isolation levels. For example, no validation is required for read committed and snapshot isolation, and only read set visibility check is needed for repeatable read. Both checks are required only for serializable isolation.

isting one in place, and only records whose valid time (i.e., a time range denoted by start and end timestamps) overlaps the logical read time of the transaction are visible. The uncommitted records are allowed to be speculatively read/ignored/updated if those records have reached the validation phase, in order to advance the processing, and not to block during the normal processing phase. But speculative processing enforces commit dependencies, which may cause cascaded abort and must be resolved before committing.

It utilizes atomic operations for updating on the valid time of records, visibility checking and conflict detection, rather than locking. Finally, a version of a record is garbagecollected (GC) if it is no longer visible to any active transaction, in a cooperative and parallel manner. That is, the worker threads running the transaction workload can remove the garbage when encountering it, which also naturally provides a parallel GC mechanism. Garbage in the never-accessed area will be collected by a dedicated GC process.

5.4.2 Latch-Free Bw-Tree

Hekaton proposes a latch-free B-tree index, called Bw-tree, which uses delta updates to make state changes, based on atomic compare-and-swap (CAS) instructions and an elastic virtual page [3] management subsystem—LLAMA. LLAMA provides a virtual page interface, on top of which logical page IDs (PIDs) are used by Bw-tree instead of pointers, which can be translated into physical address based on a mapping table. This allows the physical address of a Bw-tree node to change on every update, without requiring the address change to be propagated to the root of the tree. In particular, delta updates are performed by prepending the update delta page to the prior page and atomically updating the mapping table, thus avoiding update-in-place which may result in costly cache invalidation especially on multi-socket environment, and preventing the in-use data from being updated simultaneously, enabling latch-free access. The delta update strategy applies to both leaf node update achieved by simply prepending a delta page to the page containing the prior leaf node, and structure modification operations (SMO) (e.g., node split and merge) by a series of non-blocking cooperative and atomic delta updates, which are participated by any worker thread encountering the uncompleted SMO. Delta pages and base page are consolidated in a later pointer, in order to relieve the search efficiency degradation caused by the long chain of delta pages. Replaced pages are reclaimed by the epoch mechanism, to protect data potentially used by other threads, from being freed too early.

---

[3] The virtual page here does not mean that used by OS. There is no hard limit on the page size, and pages grow by prepending "delta pages" to the base page.

5.4.3 Siberia in Hekaton

Project Siberia [40] aims to enable Hekaton to automatically and transparently maintain cold data on the cheaper secondary storage, allowing more data fit in Hekaton than the available memory. Instead of maintaining an LRU list like H-Store Anti-Caching, Siberia performs offline classification of hot and cold data by logging tuple accesses first, and then analyzing them offline to predict the top K hot tuples with the highest estimated access frequencies, using an efficient parallel classification algorithm based on exponential smoothing. The record access logging method incurs less overhead than an LRU list in terms of both memory and CPU usage. In addition, to relieve the memory overhead caused by the evicted tuples, Siberia does not store any additional information in memory about the evicted tuples (e.g., keys in the index, evicted table) other than the multiple variable-size Bloom filters and adaptive range filters that are used to filter the access to disk. Besides, in order to make it transactional even when a transaction accesses both hot and cold data, it transactionally coordinates between hot and cold stores so as to guarantee consistency, by using a durable update memo to temporarily record notices that specify the current status of cold records [40].

5.5 HyPer/ScyPer Data Base Systems

HyPer [35] or its distributed version ScyPer [41] is designed as a hybrid OLTP and OLAP high performance in-memory database with utmost utilization of modern hardware features. OLTP transactions are executed sequentially in a lock-less style which is first advocated in and parallelism is achieved by logically partitioning the database and admitting multiple partition-constrained transactions in parallel. It can yield an unprecedentedly high transaction rate, as high as 100,000 per second [35]. The superior performance is attributed to the low latency of data access in inmemory databases, the effectiveness of the space-efficient Adaptive Radix Tree and the use of stored transaction procedures. OLAP queries are conducted on a consistent snapshot achieved by the virtual memory snapshot mechanism based on hardware-supported shadow pages, which is an efficient concurrency control model with low maintenance overhead. In addition, HyPer adopts a dynamic query compilation scheme, i.e., the SQL queries are first compiled into assembly code, which can then be executed directly using an optimizing Just-in-Time (JIT) compiler provided by LLVM. This query evaluation follows a datacentric paradigm by applying as many operations on a data object as possible, thus keeping data in the registers as long as possible to achieve register-locality.

The distributed version of HyPer, i.e., ScyPer [41], adopts a primary-secondary architecture, where the primary node is responsible for all the OLTP requests and also acts as the entry point for OLAP queries, while secondary nodes are only used to execute the OLAP queries. To synchronize the updates from the primary node to the secondary nodes, the logical redo log is multicast to all secondary nodes using Pragmatic General Multicast protocol (PGM), where the redo log is replayed to catch up with the primary. Further, the secondary nodes can subscribe to specific partitions, thus allowing the provisioning of secondary nodes for specific partitions and enabling a more flexible multi-tenancy model. In the current version of ScyPer, there is only one primary node, which holds all the data in memory, thus bounding the database size or the transaction processing power to one server.

Next, we will elaborate on HyPer's snapshot mechanism, register-conscious compilation scheme and the ART indexing.

5.5.1 Snapshot in HyPer

HyPer constructs a consistent snapshot by fork-ing a child process (via fork() system call) with its own copied virtual memory space [42], which involves no software concurrency control mechanism but the hardware-assisted virtual memory management with little maintenance overhead. By fork-ing a child process, all the data in the parent process is virtually "copied" to the child process. It is however quite light-weight as the copyon- write mechanism will trigger the real copying only when some process is trying to modify a page, which is achieved by the OS and the memory management unit (MMU). As reported in [43], the page replication is efficient as it can be done in 2 ms. Consequently, a consistent snapshot can be constructed efficiently for the OLAP queries without heavy synchronization cost.

In [44], four snapshot mechanisms were benchmarked: software-based Tuple Shadowing which generates a new version when a tuple is modified, software-based Twin Tuple which always keeps two versions of each tuple, hardware based Page Shadowing used by HyPer, and HotCold Shadowing which combines Tuple Shadowing and hardware-supported Page Shadowing by clustering update-intensive objects. The study shows that Page Shadowing is superior in terms of OLTP performance, OLAP query response time and memory consumption. The most time-consuming task in the creation of a snapshot in the Page Shadowing mechanism is the copying of a process's page table, which can be reduced by using huge page (2 MB per page on x86) for cold data. The hot or cold data is monitored and clustered with a hardware-assisted approach by reading/resetting the young and dirty flags of a page. Compression is applied on cold data to further improve the performance of OLAP workload and reduce memory consumption.

Snapshot is not only used for OLAP queries, but also for long-running transactions, as these long-running transactions will block other short good-natured transactions in the serial execution model. In HyPer, these ill-natured transactions are identified and tentatively executed on a child process with a consistent snapshot, and the changes made by these transactions are effected by issuing a deterministic "apply transaction", back to the main database process. The apply transaction validates the execution of the tentative transaction, by checking that all reads performed on the snapshot are identical to what would have been read on the main database if view serializability is required, or by checking the writes on the snapshot are disjoint from the writes by all transactions on the main database after the snapshot was created if the snapshot isolation is required. If the validation succeeds, it applies the writes to the main database state. Otherwise an abort is reported to the client.

5.5.2 Register-Conscious Compilation

To process a query, HyPer translates it into compact and efficient machine code using the LLVM compiler framework [45], rather than using the classical iterator-based query processing model. The HyPer JIT compilation model is designed to avoid function calls by extending recursive function calls into a code fragment loop, thus resulting in better code locality and data locality (i.e., temporal locality for CPU registers), because each code fragment performs all actions on a tuple within one execution pipeline during which the tuple is kept in the registers, before materializing the result into the memory for the next pipeline. As an optimized high-level language compiler (e.g., C++) is slow, HyPer uses the LLVM compiler framework to generate portable assembler code for an SQL query. In particular, when processing an SQL query, it is first processed as per normal, i.e., the query is parsed, translated and optimized into an algebraic logical plan. However, the algebraic logical plan is not translated into an executable physical plan as in the conventional scheme, but instead compiled into an imperative program (i.e., LLVM assembler code) which can then be executed directly using the JIT compiler provided by LLVM. Nevertheless, the complex part of query processing (e.g., complex data structure management, sorting) is still written in C++, which is pre-compiled. As the LLVM code can directly call the native C++ method without additional wrapper, C++ and LLVM interact with each other without performance penalty [45]. However, there is a trade-off between defining functions, and inlining code in one compact code fragment, in terms of code cleanness, the size of the executable file, efficiency, etc.

5.5.3 ART Indexing

HyPer uses an adaptive radix tree [46] for efficient indexing. The property of the radix tree guarantees that the keys are ordered bit-wise lexicographically, making it possible for range scan, prefix lookup, etc. Larger span of radix tree can decrease the tree height linearly, thus speeding up the search process, but increase the space consumption exponentially. ART achieves both space and time efficiency by adaptively using different inner node sizes with the same, relatively large span, but different fan-out. Specifically, there are four types of inner nodes with a span of 8 bits but different capacities: Node4, Node16, Node48 and Node256, which are named according to their maximum capacity of storing child node pointers. In particular, Node4/Node16 can store up to 4/16 child pointers and uses an array of length 4/16 for sorted keys and another array of the same length for child pointers. Node48 uses a 256-element array to directly index key bits to the pointer array with capacity of 48, while Node256 is simply an array of 256 pointers as normal radix tree node, which is used to store between 49 to 256 entries. Lazy expansion and path compression techniques are adopted to further reduce the memory consumption.

5.6 SAP HANA Data Base System

SAP HANA [23] is a distributed in-memory database featured for the integration of OLTP and OLAP [47], and the unification of structured (i.e., relational table), semi-structured (i.e., graph) and unstructured data (i.e., text) processing. All the data is kept in memory as long as there is enough space available, otherwise entire data objects (e.g., tables or partitions) are unloaded from memory and reloaded into memory when they are needed again.

HANA has the following features:

- It supports both row- and column-oriented stores for relational data, in order to optimize different query workloads. Furthermore, it exploits columnar data layout for both efficient OLAP and OLTP by adding two levels of delta data structures to alleviate the inefficiency of insertion and deletion operations in columnar data structures.
- It provides rich data analytics functionality by offering multiple query language interfaces (e.g., standard SQL, SQLScript, MDX, WIPE, FOX and R), which makes it easy to push down more application semantics into the data management layer, thus avoiding heavy data transfer cost.
- It supports temporal queries based on the Timeline Index naturally as data is versioned in HANA.
- It provides snapshot isolation based on multi-version concurrency control, transaction semantics based on optimized two-phase commit protocol (2PC), and fault-tolerance by logging and periodic checkpointing into GPFS file system.

We will elaborate only on the first three features, as the other feature is a fairly common technique used in the literature.

5.6.1 Relational Stores

SAP HANA supports both row- and column-oriented physical representations of relational tables. Row store is beneficial for heavy updates and inserts, as well as point queries that are common in OLTP, while column store is ideal for OLAP applications as they usually access all values of a column together, and few columns at a time. Another benefit for column-oriented representation is that it can utilize compression techniques more effectively and efficiently. In HANA, a table/partition can be configured to be either in the row store or in the column store, and it can also be re-structured from one store to the other.

HANA also provides a storage advisor to recommend the optimal representation based on data and query characteristics by taking both query cost and compression rate into consideration. As a table/partition only exists in either a row store or a column store, and both have their own weaknesses, HANA designs a three-level column-oriented unified table structure, consisting of L1-delta, L2-delta and main store, to provide efficient support for both OLTP and OLAP workloads, which shows that column store can be deployed efficiently for OLTP as well [41]. In general, a tuple is first stored in L1-delta in row format, then propagated to L2-delta in column format and finally merged with the main store with heavier compression. The whole process of the three stages is called a lifecycle of a tuple in HANA term.

5.6.2 Rich Data Analytics Support

HANA supports various programming interfaces for data analytics (i.e., OLAP), including standard SQL for generic data management functionality, and more specialized languages such as SQL script, MDX, FOX, WIPE and R. While SQL queries are executed in the same manner as in a traditional database, other specialized queries have to be transformed. These queries are first parsed into an intermediate abstract data flow model called "calculation graph model", where source nodes represent persistent or intermediate tables and inner nodes reflect logical operators performed by these queries, and then transformed into execution plans similar to that of an SQL query. Unlike other systems, HANA supports R scripting as part of the system to enable better optimization of ad-hoc data analytics jobs. Specifically, R scripts can be embedded into a custom operator in the calculation graph. When an R operator is to be executed, a separate R runtime is invoked using the Rserve package. As the column format of HANA column-oriented table is similar to R's vector-oriented dataframe, there is little overhead in the transformation from table to dataframe. Data transfer is achieved via shared memory, which is an efficient inter-process communication (IPC) mechanism. With the help of RICE package, it only needs to copy once to make the data available for the R process, i.e., it just copies the data from the database to the shared memory section, and the R runtime can access the data from the shared memory section directly.

5.6.3 Temporal Query

HANA supports temporal queries, such as temporal aggregation, time travel and temporal join, based on a unified index structure called the Timeline Index [48]. For every logical table, HANA keeps the current version of the table in a Current Table and the whole history of previous versions in a Temporal Table, accompanied with a Timeline Index to facilitate temporal queries. Every tuple of the Temporal Table carries a valid interval, from its commit time to its last valid time, at which some transaction invalidates that value. Transaction Time in HANA is represented by discrete, monotonically increasing versions. Basically, the Timeline Index maps each version to all the write events (i.e., records in the Temporal Table) that committed before or at that version. A Timeline Index consists of an Event List and a Version Map, where the Event List keeps track of every invalidation or validation event, and the Version Map keeps track of the sequence of events that can be seen by each version of the database. Consequently due to the fact that all visible rows of the Temporal Table at every point in time are tracked, temporal queries can be implemented by scanning Event List and Version Map concurrently. To reduce the full scan cost for constructing a temporal view, HANA augments the difference-based Timeline Index with a number of complete view representations, called checkpoints, at a specific time in the history. In particular, a checkpoint is a bit vector with length equal to the number of rows in the Temporal Table, which represents the visible rows of the Temporal Table at a certain time point (i.e., a certain version). With the help of checkpoints, a temporal view at a certain time can be obtained by scanning from the latest checkpoint before that time, rather than scanning from the start of the Event List each time.

References

[1] Avi Silberschatz, Peter Baer and Galvin Greg Gagne, Operating System Concepts, 10th ed., John Wiley & Sons, 2013, p. 10.

[2] David A. Patterson and John L.Hennessy, Computer Organization and Design. The hardware/software interface, 5th ed., Elsevier, 2014, p. 378.

[3] B. Lincoln, Digital Electronics, 1/e, Pearson India, 2014.

[4] ITL Limited ITL Education Solutions Limited, Introduction to Computer Science, Pearson Education India, 2011.

[5] A. N. Kamthane and R. Kamal, Computer Programming and IT, Pearson India, 2012.

[6] J. S. Warford, Computer systems, 5th ed., Jones & Bartlett Learning, 2016.

[7] S. Haldar and A. Aravind, Operating Systems, Pearson India, 2009.

[8] R. Sedgewick and K. Wayne, Computer Science: An Interdisciplinary Approach, Addison-Wesley Professional, 2016.

[9] R. e. O'Neill, Learning Linux Binary Analysis, 2016.

[10] Oracle, "Locality Groups Overview," 28 09 2017. [Online].

[11] M. K. McKusick, G. V. Neville-Neil and R. N. Watson, "The Slab Allocator," in The Design and Implementation of the FreeBSD Operating System,2nd ed., Addison-Wesley Professional, 2014.

[12] E. C. Foster and S. V. Godbole, Database Systems, Apress, 2014.

[13] J. G. Raghu Ramakrishnan, Database Management Systems, 3th ed., McGraw-Hill, 2002.

[14] S. Naik, Concepts of Database Management System, Pearson India, 2013.

[15] G. S. M. Calzarossa, "Workload characterization: a survey," Proceedings of the IEEE (Volume: 81, Issue: 8, Aug 1993), pp. 1136 - 1150, 1993.

[16] H. Garcia-Molina, J.Ullman, J.Widom, Database Systems: The complete Book, Second Edition, New Jersey: Prentice Hall, 2009.

[17] R. A. Steward and J. Goodson, The Data Access Handbook: Achieving Optimal Database Application Performance and Scalability, Prentice Hall, 2009.

[18] D. Vadala, Managing RAID on Linux, O'Reilly Media, Inc, 2002.

[19] Oracle Corporation, MySQL 5.7 Reference Manual, Oracle Corporation, 2018.

[20] S. Pachev, Understanding MySQL Internals, O'Reilly Media, Inc, 2007.

[21] H. Zhang, G. Chen, B. Chin Ooi, K. Tan, M. Zhang, "In-Memory Big Data Management and Processing: A Survey", IEEE Transactions on Knowledge and Data Engineering, (Volume: 27, Issue: 7, July 1 2015) .

[22] Gianlucca O.Puglia, Avelino F.Zorzo, Cesar A.F. de Rose, Taciano D.Perez, and Dejan Milojicic, "Non-Volatile Memory File Systems: A Survey". IEEE Access, Vol. 7, 2019.

[23] V. Sikka, F. Farber, A. Goel, and W. Lehner, "SAP HANA: The evolution from a modern main-memory data platform to an enterprise application platform", Proc. VLDB Endowment, vol. 6, pp. 1184–1185, 2013.

[24] M. Stonebraker and A. Weisberg, "The voltDB main memory DBMs," IEEE Data Eng. Bull., vol. 36, no. 2, Jun. 2013.

[25] T. Lahiri, M.-A. Neimat, and S. Folkman, "Oracle timesten: An in-memory database for enterprise applications," IEEE Data Eng. Bull., vol. 36, no. 2, pp. 6–13, Jun. 2013.

[26] J. Lindström, V. Raatikka, J. Ruuth, P. Soini, and K. Vakkila, "IBM solidDB: In-memory database optimized for extreme speed and availability," IEEE Data Eng. Bull., vol. 36, no. 2, pp. 14–20, Jun. 2013.

[27] V. Raman, G. Attaluri, R. Barber, N. Chainani, D. Kalmuk, V. KulandaiSamy, J. Leenstra, S. Lightstone, S. Liu, G. M. Lohman, T. Malkemus, R. Mueller, I. Pandis, B. Schiefer, D. Sharpe, R. Sidle, A. Storm and L.Zhang, "DB2 with BLU acceleration: So much more than just a column store" Proc. VLDB Endowment, vol. 6, pp. 1080–1091, 2013.

[28] C. Diaconu, C. Freedman, E. Ismert, P.-A. Larson, P. Mittal, R. Stonecipher, N. Verma, and M. Zwilling, "Hekaton: SQL server's memory-optimized OLTP engine," in Proc. ACM SIGMOD Int. Conf. Manag. Data, 2013, pp. 1243–1254.

[29] R. Kallman, H. Kimura, J. Natkins, A. Pavlo, A. Rasin, S. Zdonik, E. P. C. Jones, S. Madden, M. Stonebraker, Y. Zhang, J. Hugg, and D. J. Abadi, "H-store: A high-performance, distributed main memory transaction processing system, " Proc. VLDB Endowment, vol. 1, pp. 1496–1499, 2008.

[30] B. Brynko, "Nuodb: Reinventing the database," Inf. Today, vol. 29, no. 9, p. 9, 2012.

[31] McObject, "extremedb database system," 2001. [Online]. Available: http:// www.mcobject.com/extremedbfamily.shtml

[32] Pivotal. (2013). Pivotal SQLFire [Online]. Available: http:// www.vmware.com/products/vfabric-sqlfire/overview.html

[33] MemSQL Inc. (2012). Memsql [Online]. Available: http://www.memsql.com/

[34] FoundationDB. (2013). Foundationdb[Online]. Available: https://foundationdb.com

[35] A. Kemper and T. Neumann, "HyPer: A hybrid OLTP & OLAP main memory database system based on virtual memory snapshots," in IEEE 27th Int. Conf. Data Eng., 2011, pp. 195–206.

[36] S. Tu, W. Zheng, E. Kohler, B. Liskov, and S. Madden, "Speedy transactions in multicore in-memory databases," in Proc. ACM Symp. Operating Syst. Prin-

ciples, 2013, pp. 18–32.

[37] P. Unterbrunner, G. Giannikis, G. Alonso, D. Fauser, and D. Kossmann, "Predictable performance for unpredictable workloads," Proc. VLDB Endowment, vol. 2, pp. 706–717, 2009.

[38] M. Grund, J. Krüger, H. Plattner, A. Zeier, P. Cudre-Mauroux, and S. Madden, "HYRISE: A main memory hybrid storage engine," Proc. VLDB Endowment, vol. 4, pp. 105–116, 2010.

[39] Oracle. (2004). MySQL cluster NDB [Online]. Available: http://www.mysql.com/

[40] A. Eldawy, J. J. Levandoski, and P. Larson, "Trekking through Siberia: Managing cold data in a memory-optimized database," in Proc. Int. Conf. Very Large Data Bases, 2014, pp. 931–942.

[41] T. Mühlbauer, W. Rödiger, A. Reiser, A. Kemper, and T. Neumann, "ScyPer: Elastic OLAP throughput on transactional data," in Proc. 2nd Workshop Data Analytics Cloud, 2013, pp. 11–15.

[42] A. Kemper and T. Neumann, "HyPer: A hybrid OLTP & OLAP main memory database system based on virtual memory snapshots," in IEEE 27th Int. Conf. Data Eng., 2011, pp. 195–206.

[43] A. Kemper and T. Neumann, "One size fits all, again! the architecture of the hybrid oltp & olap database management system hyper," in Proc. 4th Int. Workshop Enabling Real-Time Bus. Intell., 2010, pp. 7–23.

[44] H. Mühe, A. Kemper, and T. Neumann, "How to efficiently snapshot transactional data: Hardware or software controlled?" in Proc. 7th Int. Workshop Data Manag. New Hardware, 2011, pp. 17–26.

[45] T. Neumann, "Efficiently compiling efficient query plans for modern hardware," Proc. VLDB Endowment, vol. 4, pp. 539–550, 2011.

[46] V. Leis, A. Kemper, and T. Neumann, "The adaptive radix tree: ARTful indexing for main-memory databases," in Proc. IEEE 29th Int. Conf. Data Eng., 2013, pp. 38–49.

[47] H. Plattner, "A common database approach for OLTP and olap USING an in-memory column database," in Proc. ACM SIGMOD Int. Conf. Manag. Data, 2009, pp. 1–2.

[48] M. Kaufmann and D. Kossmann, "Storing and processing temporal data in a main memory column store," Proc. VLDB Endowment, vol. 6, pp. 1444–1449, 2013.

[49] Intel® 64 and IA-32 Architectures Software Developer's Manual Volume 3A: System Programming Guide, Part 1. https://www.intel.es/content/www/es/es/architecture-and-technology/64-ia-32-architectures-software-developer-vol-3a-part-1-manual.html

[50] AMD64 Architecture, Programmer's Manual, Volume 2: System Programming, https://www.amd.com/system/files/TechDocs/24593.pdf

[51] F. Chang, J. Dean, S. Ghemawat, W. C. Hsieh, D. A. Wallach, M. Burrows, T. Chandra, A. Fikes, and R. E. Gruber, "Bigtable: A distributed storage system for structured data," ACM Trans. Compu. Syst., vol. 26, pp. 4:1–4:26, 2008.

[52] S. Sanfilippo and P. Noordhuis. (2009). Redis [Online]. Available:

http://redis.io

[53] J. Ousterhout, P. Agrawal, D. Erickson, C. Kozyrakis, J. Leverich, D. Mazieres, S. Mitra, A. Narayanan, G. Parulkar, M. Rosenblum, S. M. Rumble, E. Stratmann, and R. Stutsman, "The case for RAMClouds: Scalable high performance storage entirely in dram," ACM SIGOPS Operating Syst. Rev., vol. 43, pp. 92–105, 2010.

[54] Q. Cai, H. Zhang, G. Chen, B. C. Ooi, and K.-L. Tan, "Memepic: Towards a database system architecture without system calls," NUS, 2014.

[55] S. Ramachandran. (2013). Bitsy graph database [Online]. Available: https://bitbucket.org/lambdazen/bitsy

[56] MongoDB Inc. (2009). Mongodb [Online]. Available: http://www.mongodb.org

[57] M. C. Brown, Getting Started with Couchbase Server. Sebastopol, CA, USA: O'Reilly Media, 2012.

[58] B. Shao, H. Wang, and Y. Li, "Trinity: A distributed graph engine on a memory cloud," in Proc. ACM SIGMOD Int. Conf. Manag. Data, 2013, pp. 505–516.

[59] S. Ramachandran. (2013). Bitsy graph database [Online]. Available: https://bitbucket.org/lambdazen/bitsy

[60] B. Bishop, A. Kiryakov, D. Ognyanoff, I. Peikov, Z. Tashev, and R. Velkov, "OWLIM: A family of scalable semantic repositories," Semantic Web, vol. 2, pp. 33–42, 2011.

[61] WhiteDB Team. (2013). Whitedb [Online]. Available: http://whitedb.org

[62] P. A. Boncz, M. Zukowski, and N. Nes, "Monetdb/x100: Hyperpipelining query execution," in Proc. CIDR, 2005, pp. 225–237.

[63] H. Chu, "MDB: A memory-mapped database and backend for openldap," in Proc. LDAPCon, 2011.

[64] Hector Garcia-Molina, "Main Memory Database Systems: An Overview". IEEE Transactions on Knowledge and Data Engineering, Vol. 4, No. 6, December.

[65] F. Li, B. C. Ooi, M. T. Özsu, and S. Wu, "Distributed data management using MapReduce," ACM Computing Surveys, vol. 46, pp. 31:1–31:42, 2014.

Printed in the United States
by Baker & Taylor Publisher Services